GW00374784

EARLY ADVERTISING ART FROM THE IMPERIAL TOBACCO COMPANY
PIPE DREAMS
EDITED BY MIKE DEMPSEY & INTRODUCED BY TIM SHACKLETON

PAVILION
MICHAEL JOSEPH

To Margaret

The publishers gratefully acknowledge the assistance of Denis Mitchell of Imperial Tobacco Limited, William Fazakerley of Ogden, Alan Dobson of John Player & Sons, David Redway and Hubert Rudman of W.D. & H.O. Wills and Michael Moorcock in the preparation of this book.



First published in Great Britain in 1982 by
Pavilion Books Limited
196 Shaftesbury Avenue London WC2H 8JL
in association with Michael Joseph Limited
44 Bedford Square London WC1B 3DU

Designed by Carroll & Dempsey Ltd., London
Colour separation, Gilchrist Bros., Leeds
Made and printed in Singapore by Tien Wah Press



Pipe dreams:
early advertising art from the Imperial Tobacco Company.
1. Imperial Tobacco Limited. 2. Commercial art.
3. Advertising—Tobacco industries—Pictorial work
I. Dempsey, Mike, II. Shackleton, Tim
659.13'14 HF6166.I/

ISBN 0-907516-12-2

The ever-increasing sales of cigarettes in the last decade of the nineteenth century moved a commentator in the trade journal *Tobacco* (1 November 1897) to wonder 'what measure of its present tremendous popularity the cigarette would have enjoyed had not the printer come to the assistance of the manufacturer with his attractive packages'. He was, of course, referring essentially to the colourful and bold design of the actual cigarette packet, but his remark has significance in a wider context. Before the century was out, manufacturers and retailers in many lines had come to recognise the central importance of 'the package' as a whole, so familiar to selling techniques today. Successful trading was coming to depend on a careful integration of product, package, advertising, trade discount, financial incentives and other commercial aspects. This was particularly evident in the British tobacco industry, where the rapid mushrooming of advertising which began in the 1880s can in part be attributed to three reasons.

W. G. PLAYER AND MEMBERS OF HIS STAFF, 1885.

The first was that the final twenty years of the nineteenth century saw manufacturers struggling in a depressed economy to capture what parts of the market they could. Advertising was a prime agent in their fight, though the curious mixture of ostentation and restraint which characterised the late Victorian mind provoked a certain amount of resistance and partially muffled its impact: in *Clayhanger*, the novelist Arnold Bennett instances 'a recently established drapers . . . whose extravagant advertising had shocked and pained the commerce of the Five Towns'. Though moral considerations and standards of decency may have been outraged in some quarters by exceptionally bold advertising, there was no doubt that it was here to stay. Its spread was encouraged by the development, from the early 1880s, of revolutionary lithographic printing techniques, which allowed poster and showcard advertising particularly to break away from the constraints of the purely typographic approach to layout which had hitherto been prevalent into the realms of full colour illustration and graphic design. Printing technology was especially significant to the tobacco industry since, as we shall see, a very large proportion of its advertising material (showcards, posters, cigarette cards etc.) was produced by one printing firm, which also manufactured much of the packaging used in the trade.

The third factor was the change in retailing techniques which the latter years of the century had witnessed. Until that time, most provisions sold for immediate personal consumption (foodstuffs, confectionery, tobacco for example) were kept loose in bulk by shopkeepers, to be measured out at the customer's request in whatever quantity he or she desired and wrapped in coarse paper or, very commonly, newspaper. Many goods were not identified by a brand name at all, and of those that were, few could boast packaging that strikes the modern eye as in any way imaginative.

Customers were not in the habit – so familiar today – of asking for a particular manufacturer's product by name; their loyalty lay towards a shop, not to a brand. All the more striking, then, were we to enter an average corner shop in, say, 1887 and see there on the shelf, amidst the sacks of potatoes, large open tins of biscuits, boxes of loose soap, hanging flitches of bacon and bundles of firelighters, the basket-patterned paper of a box of Wills' Double Daffodil cigarettes, silver-edged and fastened with a twinkling silver star. Our eyes might rove over the colourful advertising showcards for branded tobacco goods displayed around the shop and its windows, and we would be aware of something novel, something eye-catching and attractive which demanded not only that we should look at it, but that we should actually buy it – even though we may not originally have intended to buy cigarettes – and continue to buy this particular and readily identifiable brand in the future if we were pleased with its quality.

Pre-packaged, standardised goods were nothing new to either customer or shopkeeper at this time: John Horniman in London had been selling sealed, branded packets of tea as early as 1826. Nor was persuasive advertising. But neither had yet been exploited to its full potential. It is well worth looking at some of the early history of the UK tobacco industry to see how the position it found itself in at the end of the nineteenth century came about. The fortunes of the Wills and Players concerns are particularly relevant: both began in modest and entirely typical ways, and both exhibited in time the combination of initiative and commercial acumen that would install them as undisputed market leaders, whose innovations called the tune for the rest of the industry.

Wills' history goes back to 1786, when Henry Overton Wills came to Bristol from Salisbury and went into partnership with one Samuel Watkins in the latter's tobacco-manufacturing business in Castle Street. Bristol has been one of the chief centres of the tobacco industry since the early days of trade with North America, and by the end of the eighteenth century tobacco from Virginia was one of the chief imports of a city which had some fourteen tobacco manufacturers. Casks of Virginia tobacco were hauled up from the quayside to the firm's small workshop, where a workforce of eight laboured at removing the leaves from the stems and preparing the tobacco for sale. At first known as Wills, Watkins & Co., the firm briefly became H.O.Wills & Co. following Watkin's retirement in 1789 before Wills joined forces with Peter Lilly, trading at 112 Redcliffe Street, to form Lilly and Wills. His two sons, William Day and Henry Overton Wills (both, incidentally, lifelong non-smokers) joined the firm in 1815 and took over full control on their father's death in 1826. The firm became known as W.D. & H.O. Wills for the first time in 1830; three years later, it took over another significant Bristol tobacco manufacturer, Ricketts, Leonard, Ricketts & Co., to become Ricketts, Wills & Co., but from 1847 the firm reverted to its 1830 title which, with only minor variations, has been used ever since. Though much of their early advertising used the possessive 'Wills's', the modern usage is 'Wills'', and this style has been adapted in this book.

JOHN PLAYER'S FIRST TOBACCO FACTORY, 1877.

John Player, however, entered the tobacco industry from the retail rather than the manufacturing side. He came to Nottingham from Essex in 1862 and set up in business on Beastmarket Hill as an agent for agricultural manures and seeds. As a side-line he sold tobacco, taking in loose tobacco in bulk as it was supplied from manufacturers like Wills and dispensing it from the jars in which it was kept into small paper packages or 'screws' for the convenience of customers buying a few pence worth of tobacco to cover their immediate needs. It was a logical step for him to cater for a customer's preference for a particular blend of tobacco by pre-packing it, and Player evidently found this trade so lucrative that in 1877 he took over a Nottingham tobacco factory that had been established in 1823 by William Wright and which, catering solely for local needs, was employing some 150 people. The bulk of his trade was in branded, pre-packed tobacco (he registered his Nottingham Castle trade mark almost as soon as he took over Wright's factory), although he was far from being the first in the country to deal in this aspect of the trade.

At least as early as 1675, branding had existed in rudimentary form, with specialist tobacconists making use of printed labels (sometimes pictorial, using the familiar negro, blackamoor or Red Indian figure) to distinguish such types of tobacco or snuff as were exclusively theirs. This not only emphasised any distinctive characteristics the product might have and enabled it to be identified *by name*, but also gave the tobacconist something to sell which was distinguishable from the common product, for which, not surprisingly, an accordingly higher price might be asked, and which was a valuable weapon in his economic competition with his rivals.

Whatever increased demand this early form of branding was capable of generating, its widespread adoption in the field of tobacco retailing had necessarily to await a considerable improvement in the manufacturers' methods of production and packing. This was not to become generally effected until the advent of the revolutionary new machinery of the last quarter of the nineteenth century. Until that time, successful selling of both loose and pre-packaged goods depended exclusively on the retailer's knowledge of the goods he was buying in from the manufacturer and his ability to perceive and cater for localised tastes: it was known, for instance, that strong shags and roll tobaccos sold well in Welsh mining communities, while the milder Virginia mixtures found greater favour in London. In the second half of the century, however, this expertise was challenged by the arrival on the market of standardised products. On New Year's Day 1847 Ricketts, Wills & Co. put on to the market two of its cut tobaccos in branded form as Best Bird's

PLAYER'S DELIVERY VEHICLES, 1920s.

Eye and Bishop Blaze. Later their initiative in branding was followed by Lambert & Butler, Hignett Bros and Cope Bros. The intention was not, as that of the early tobacconists had been, to give the products exclusivity; rather, by standardisation and ready identification in the public eye, they aimed to make them accessible to a mass market across the country. By this means, as Robert Opie suggests, 'the manufacturer can make direct contact with the individual customer. He himself labels the package, places his name on it, chooses the name for the product, and can add, if he wishes, his own assurance of its quality and other virtues'. Though the tobacco trade was not revolutionised overnight by this pioneering action (weighing, wrapping and labelling were still laborious manual tasks and an efficient machine for performing these duties would not be available for upwards of thirty years) the stranglehold of the retail tobacconists had effectively been breached and branded tobacco could now be sold in non-specialist outlets by shopkeepers without an expert's knowledge of the commodity to customers expecting a standardised product wherever they bought it. In part this enabled the total number of retailers and dealers in tobacco and snuff in the U.K. to rise from 122,460 in 1825 to 215,437 in 1850 and 296,718 in 1880. The development of branding and pre-packaging by the manufacturers gradually brought about the demise of the trade in retailer's own brands, though naturally the former was still dependent on the latter for the distribution of his products. Again, despite the growth towards nationally available products, there was still some scope in catering towards strong local tastes; right up to the early 1960s, in fact, some chewing tobaccos popular among South Wales miners (who could not, of course, smoke underground) lingered on the Wills price list.

As a result of the generally improved prosperity and trading conditions of the 1850s competition among tobacco manufacturers increased. As well as the gradual rise of branding, the decade saw a modest but steady growth in advertising and promotional activity: a letter of 1855 in Wills' archives shows them supplying a tobacco dealer in Leek, Staffordshire, with 'some showcards for your window' (these were printed in two colours, probably by Mardon's of Bristol) while in 1860 they were subsidising a tobacconist who mentioned the firm's name in his weekly advertisements in the *Inverness Courier*. In this interim period of tobacco advertising, some of the promotional techniques of other consumer industries were copied by tobacco manufacturers – they noticed, for instance, how brewers publicised their name and products in engraved glass in public houses and before long display cabinets and glass panels carrying appropriate slogans were being made available to retail tobacconists. As smoking became more socially acceptable as the century moved towards its final quarter (the briar pipe began to replace the picturesque but humble clay, smoking carriages were introduced on railways and popular writers such as Carlyle, Dickens, Thackeray, Tennyson and Kingsley extolled the virtues and delights of smoking) so branding increased. Yet very little was as yet being spent on advertising; as late as 1880 only 0.2 pence per lb of tobacco sold by Wills was so deployed, and this in a year

WILLS' BEDMINSTER FACTORY.

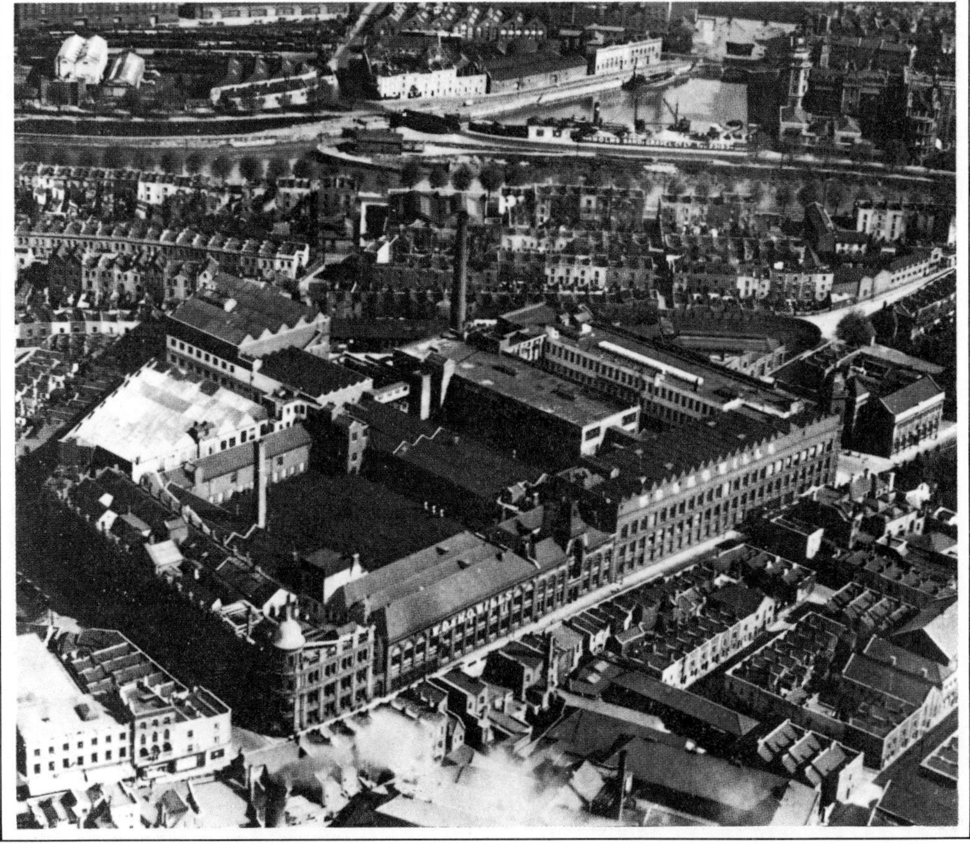

when Wills despatched 2,895,000 lb of tobacco. An advertising budget of under £2,500 per annum in this period, however, indicates not so much any unwillingness on the part of a major tobacco company to exploit the medium but rather the higher relative costs of other, more fundamental aspects of tobacco manufacture and also the surprising cheapness of printing and the ready availability of space in newspapers and on billboards. It was advertising of this localised, inexpensive kind, rather than the extensive and spectacular national campaigns of companies such as the soap manufacturers A. & F. Pears, which the ever-increasing non-specialist outlets demanded and got, catering as they did directly to the man in the street.

Between 1880 and 1901, though, a series of events precipitated not just a remarkable turnaround in the tobacco advertising, but also dramatically affected the subsequent development of the industry. The first came in 1881, when James A. Bonsack of Salem, Virginia, patented a cigarette-making machine far in advance technically of anything which had preceded it. After initial teething trouble had been ironed out, Bonsack brought his machine in 1883 to an exhibition in Paris where it was inspected by Harry Wills, who immediately recognised the machine's potential for the mass production of cigarettes. In April Bonsack demonstrated it at Wills' Redcliffe Street works in Bristol and within a month had sold exclusive rights on the machine in the U.K. to Wills for £4,000. By the beginning of the following year the Bonsack machine was in production and further machines were on order.

The Bonsack gave Wills a tremendous advantage in cigarette production over their rivals, although the public were relatively slow to catch on to the new products it made available to them, due to the fact that, ounce for ounce, tobacco in cigarette form was considerably more expensive than pipe tobacco – an important factor for all but the highest echelons of society. An outbreak of price-cutting among the major tobacco companies in 1887 impressed on Wills the advantages of low-priced, machine-made cigarettes and in June 1888 the Board made the monumental decision to bring on to the market two new brands of cigarette – one strong, the other mild – retailing at five for 1d. The names chosen – hitherto used for two minor brands of export-only tobacco – were Wild Woodbine and Cinderella. In the five months of that year during which Woodbine and Cinderella were marketed nearly five million were sold; by 1891 the annual figure was up to 84,470,750 and the penny cigarettes were outselling Wills' other brands by more than two to one.

THE BONSACK CIGARETTE MACHINE.

The experiment was an astonishing success, and yet it was achieved without any major promotion: Woodbines, Melville Wills was to write some years later, would sell 'themselves to a very large extent'. But Wills, having opened up the market for penny cigarettes, were not to enjoy its exclusive favours for long, though they retained the lion's share. In 1893 John Player & Sons installed an American-designed Elliot cigarette machine, while two years later Lambert & Butler began to use a Luddington machine, also of American origin. Other manufacturers followed suit, and they were not necessarily the giants of the industry: even the diminutive firm of W. & F. Faulkner of London, with annual sales running at less than a tenth of Wills', bought a Luddington in 1897.

Competition in all areas of the tobacco industry increased dramatically, and this became particularly noticeable in the amount of cash, energy and imagination being devoted to advertising as the century drew to its close. Wills spent £2,000 on campaigns in Liverpool and Birmingham for Diamond Queen cigarettes in 1897; £5,000 on Gold Flake the following year – in addition to the customary advertising budget for newspapers and showcards. Player's spent upwards of £20,000 a year in this area (or so claimed one of Wills' own managers, urging his directors to put real money behind their advertising and not treat it 'in a timorous, half-hearted way') and the same man estimated that extensive current campaigns for Ogden's 3d cigarettes had cost £100,000. These two firms were making considerable inroads into Wills' share of the market and Ogden's methods in particular aroused considerable professional jealousy among their rivals: by 1899 this 'tinpot firm' (to quote a disgruntled Wills traveller) was ploughing some 25% of its net profits back into advertising and making use of some exceptionally imaginative point-of-sale material. The message was clear. 'We must go in for big scale advertising – whole pages of newspapers – not fiddly cards', wrote another Wills salesman in his report.

JOHN PLAYER'S FIRST SHOP IN LATER YEARS.

This latter remark – well-intentioned and in the circumstances quite reasonable – in the long run proved short-sighted. It referred to Wills' practice, dating from 1887, of placing pieces of card (known as stiffeners) in the paper packets to give added protection to the cigarettes. Between 1887 and 1893 these small cards bore advertising for Wills' other tobacco products, often in the form of reproductions of posters, showcards and packages. In 1895 the subject matter was changed to scenes of 'Naval and Military' interest, to be followed later in the year by 'Soldiers' and 'Ships'. Thus began the cigarette card craze. They attracted widespread popularity among smokers, and became – as did the many other individual series which followed – highly collectable items and a strong form of indirect promotion, to be copied in time by other firms. Cigarette cards were issued by many companies right up to the early months of World War II when government restrictions on the use of board caused them to be withdrawn.

Despite what their travellers repeatedly said, and although extra money was made available for special local pro-

TWO OF WILLS' EARLIEST PICTORIAL CIGARETTE CARDS.

motions or for advertising products whose sales were temporarily flagging, the cautious directors of Wills did not ordain any lavish expenditure on advertising, and this was true of most of the other manufacturers – with the exception of Ogden's. They probably felt that once cheap machine-made cigarettes had captured a fair share of the market, the objective was not to increase total consumption but instead to persuade smokers to change from one brand to another. It is true to say, though, that the turn of the century saw much more colourful, attractive advertising being employed, particularly in the form of showcards for use within retail outlets. Of particular interest is the fact that one firm, Mardon, Son and Hall, was responsible for producing such material for almost the whole of the U.K. tobacco industry.

Mardon's were a long-established Bristol printers; in 1893, the year they moved to the new, purpose-built Caxton Works in Temple Gate from older premises in Milk Street, they offered employment to some 600 workers. By the year of Queen Victoria's Diamond Jubilee this figure had doubled, making Mardon's one of the biggest printers in the British

Isles. Significantly, they had long been specialists in the manufacture of cardboard boxes, and indeed claimed to have introduced the use of such packaging in many trades. They were a progressive firm, and made extensive use of modern plant; in Milk Street they had experimented with a collotype printing process which produced some beautiful specimens, but because of problems caused by the damp English climate, they turned eventually to chromolithography, installing their first Miehle machine in 1895. Mardon's were involved with Wills for many years; they printed the first of millions and millions of card cigarette boxes and paper packets for them in 1883 and had been responsible for labels and simple showcards even earlier. Their experience in working cardboard stood them in good stead for the manufacturing of cigarette packets (called cases in the trade). In 1890 Richard Dalton of Mardon's, in collaboration with Harry Wills, invented and patented a machine capable of making cases for Woodbine 5s or Gold Flake 10s at the respective rates of 2200 and 1700 an hour. In 1895 Wills loaned Mardon's £500 for the purchase of a further ten case-making machines to cater for the needs of other tobacco manufacturers and took a royalty on all cases sold. By 1897, Mardon's were fulfilling orders for almost all the tobacco companies: Wills, Ogden, Clarke, Anstie, Churchman, Hignett, Gloag, Baker, Godfrey Phillips, T. S. S., Hudden, Adkin, the American Tobacco Company, Bell, Kinnear, Edwards Ringer & Biggs, Hill, Archer, Morris, Pritchard & Burton, Fraenkel, Mitchell, Gallaher, Hodge, H. J. Nathan, Fryer & Sons, Fryer & Coultman, Smith, Strauss of Bloemfontein, Player & Sons, Mason, Robinson & Sons, Robinson & Barnsdale, Muratti, Kriegsfield, Macdonald, Harvey & Davy, J. Biggs, Taddy, Cope, Lambert & Butler, Banks & James, Brankston, Lloyd, Milligan, Faulkner et al.

They had the necessary equipment and expertise to produce the frequently elaborate showcards requested by the

DETAIL OF A DIE-CUT SHOWCARD PRODUCED FOR OGDEN'S ROBIN CIGARETTES IN 1929.

IN PRE-WORLD WAR I DAYS EXPRESS TRAINS HAD THE SAME EXCITING IMAGE FOR ADVERTISERS THAT JET TRAVEL HAD IN THE 1950s AND 60s.

tobacco industry. Often these required complicated colour impositions, special finishes, cutting-out and shaping. Many famous names figure among those commissioned by Mardon's Advertising Department (for many years in the capable hands of A. L. M. Britton) to produce designs for showcards and other advertising material. In pre-World War I days we find Tom Browne, H. M. Brock, Cecil Aldin, W. L. Wyllie, John Hassall, Caton Woodville and Lawson Wood; in later years they were joined by Lucy Kemp-Welch, W. Scott, Charles Pears, Frank Dadd, Arthur Wardle, Lionel Edwards, Stanhope Forbes, A. D. McCormick, F. M. Bennett, Christopher Clark, Gyrth Russell, Septimus Scott, H. M. Bateman and Will Owen. Additionally, Mardon's would have had at any given time some fifty or sixty artists working in-house. Roughly half were designers and lettering artists, the others being chromo artists whose great skills were used to transfer designs on to the lithographic blocks used on the printing machines. A dozen or more blocks – each of a separate colour – might be used for a single showcard, four for a cigarette case; the coloured inks, incidentally, were ground and made up by Mardon's themselves.

In the forty years or so preceding World War I, much use was also made of enamel signs in more permanent locations in the open air, such as on tobacconists' shop fronts or on railway stations, where the low rentals for leasing space made them a cheap and durable form of advertising. Many survived until after World War II, when their very permanence proved their downfall, since they could not offer the versatility and convenience of printed paper posters which could easily be taken down or pasted over once they became obsolete. Most enamelled tobacco advertisements were simple: rectangular, brightly coloured and boldly lettered, usually with the name of the brand alone, though this could be relieved by a representation of the cigarette or tobacco packet or slogans like 'Player's Please – It's The Tobacco That Counts', and 'Ogden's St Bruno – The Tobacco That Won't Be Hurried'. The Chromographic Enamel Co. of Wolverhampton are known to have made a number of enamel signs for Wills, while Stainton & Hulme of Birmingham did work for Player's and the Patent Enamel Co. of Birmingham and London made shop facia plates for Ogden's with a wood grain finish and carrying advertising for Ogden's products alongside the name of the proprietor. Brilliant Signs Ltd. of Shepherds Bush were a particularly important firm for the manufacture of many kinds of advertising signs.

WILLS' ADVERTISING SIGNS BEING MADE IN THE FACTORY OF BRILLIANT SIGNS LTD.

The new century dawned with a far greater threat to individual British tobacco companies than that provided by the cheap brands or advertising campaigns of their business rivals. The clouds were gathering on the other side of the Atlantic in the guise of the giant American Tobacco Company, an aggressively modern organisation which had reached its pre-eminent position by forcing lesser rivals out of business, making full use of modern plant such as the Bonsack machine and adopting lavish advertising methods. Now, though its products had been marketed in the U.K. for some years, it was turning its eye towards international expansion. The storm broke over Liverpool in September 1901, when A.T.C.'s President, James Buchanan Duke, bought out Ogden's for £818,000; he claimed that his company 'had set aside for the active business efforts they intended to make of [sic] capturing the English and European trade a sum of £6,000,000.' Duke then travelled south to Nottingham, but his offer for the Player business was refused. While he was considering his next move the initiative passed from his hands, and on 19 September a meeting of representatives of thirteen of the leading British tobacco manufacturers was hastily convened to discuss the situation. They decided to present a united front to the threat of invasion by amalgamating; on 3 October a provisional agreement to form a joint company was reached, and by the end of the month this had been ratified. The Imperial Tobacco Company was formally incorporated on 10 December and the following day its directors met for the first time, with Sir William Henry Wills in the chair. Within four months, the whole structure of the U.K. tobacco industry had been radically altered, but few could say the move was entirely unsuspected: Wills had been aware of the threat from A.T.C. as early as 1894, and between then and 1898 amalgamation with the other companies (and with A.T.C.) had been discussed at Board level at least three times. The battle between the two tobacco giants raged for nine months. A.T.C. pumped vast sums of money into Ogden's and slashed prices, hoping to provoke Imperial Tobacco into engaging in a price-cutting war, but they could not make a profit out of customers who knew all too well that the low prices would soon revert to their previous level if A.T.C. obtained full control of the U.K. market.

As a counter measure I.T.C. announced plans to carry the war into the enemy's camp by exporting goods to the U.S.A. and selling them in direct competition with the products of A.T.C. After this, the American offensive rapidly collapsed; in September 1902, only a year after the initial invasion, A.T.C. agreed to sell the ailing Ogden's concern to I.T.C. and to terminate their business interests in the U.K. tobacco industry. A.T.C. were to market I.T.C.'s brands in the U.S.A., and vice versa in the U.K.; they would also have representation on the Board of I.T.C.

THE ANGLO-AMERICAN 'TOBACCO WAR' OF 1901-2 GENERATED A GOOD DEAL OF COMMENT IN THE PRESS. THIS CONTEMPORARY CARTOON ECHOES THE COLONIALISM OF EARLIER YEARS.

"WHAT? YOU YOUNG YANKEE-NOODLE, STRIKE YOUR OWN FATHER!"

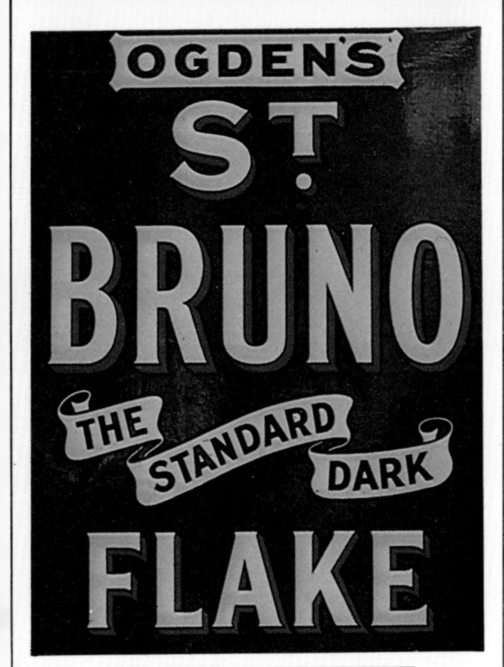


ENAMEL SIGN FOR OGDEN'S ST. BRUNO TOBACCO.

The effect of the formation of the Imperial Tobacco Company was not a great one as far as the advertising activities of its constituents was concerned. Between them, concentrated among Wills, Player's and Ogden's, they had some 70% of the U.K. tobacco market. As has already been remarked, advertising tends to make consumers switch between brands rather than increase their total consumption. Since I.T.C. already held the three leading brands – Woodbine (of which 5,000 million were smoked in 1907, far more than all the other I.T.C. brands put together), Player's Medium and Wills' Gold Flake – there was no point in sanctioning increased advertising expenditure at this stage. With Wills also holding 70% of I.T.C.'s ordinary share capital, that branch's cautious approach to advertising was the policy for the group as a whole. And though Wills' advertising budget rose from £41,000 in 1905 to £52,000 in 1913, when we consider that this represented respectively 0.7d and 0.4d per pound of tobacco sold it can clearly be seen that in real terms the amount of advertising outlay was actually declining in the years leading up to World War I. It is interesting to note, however, that this period saw advertising taken out of the hands of the major companies themselves and placed instead with professional agencies. This innovation did not produce any marked changes in approach, though a certain amount of rationalisation took place: advertising in Sunday newspapers was dropped in 1907, and the role of posters and showcards in relation to sales promotion as a whole (e.g. the use of coupons, price cutting, cigarette cards, bonus schemes etc) seems to have been more thoroughly co-ordinated than in the days of independence.

This comfortably monopolistic situation was gradually eroded in the years following World War I, and advertising activities among the members of I.T.C. changed as a result. To begin with, the 1920s saw the emergence of strong competition in the now dominant cigarette market from outside firms such as Carreras, Godfrey Phillips, J. Wix & Sons and Gallahers, among whom the distribution of coupons with top brands was a key weapon in weaning customers away from I.T.C. New forms of advertising were being introduced which spelt the end of the heyday of showcards and enamel signs, and the rapid spread of popular daily newspapers saw press advertising in the ascendancy. In 1926 Wills invested in two large neon signs, both in London: one, costing £750 and rented at £650 per annum, urged passers-by in Hammersmith Broadway to 'Always Ask For Wills's Gold Flake', while another, costing slightly less and sited in the Holloway Road, read simply 'Wills's Gold Flake Cigarettes'. In 1927 short sketches were transmitted on Radio Luxembourg featuring familiar characters from press advertising, Mr. Gold and Mr. Flake and Captain Capstan. The following year bus tickets issued by the London General Omnibus Company bore advertising for I.T.C. cigarettes, while in 1930 Mr. Gold and Mr. Flake appeared for the first time on the silver screen in a silent film commercial. Most extraordinary of all was the offer from a small aviation company to advertise Gold Flake by sky-writing the words in smoke; unfortunately, though only £250 was asked for this service, Wills declined the offer, pointing out rather frostily that such an advertisement would be of 'a temporary nature' and 'would afford amusement only'. Player's, however, were more amenable to this particularly spectacular form of promotion and Nottinghamshire people may recall the words 'Player's Please' appearing high above their heads in the mid-1930s.

MR GOLD AND MR FLAKE APPEARED IN MANY PRESS ADVERTISEMENTS BETWEEN THE WARS.

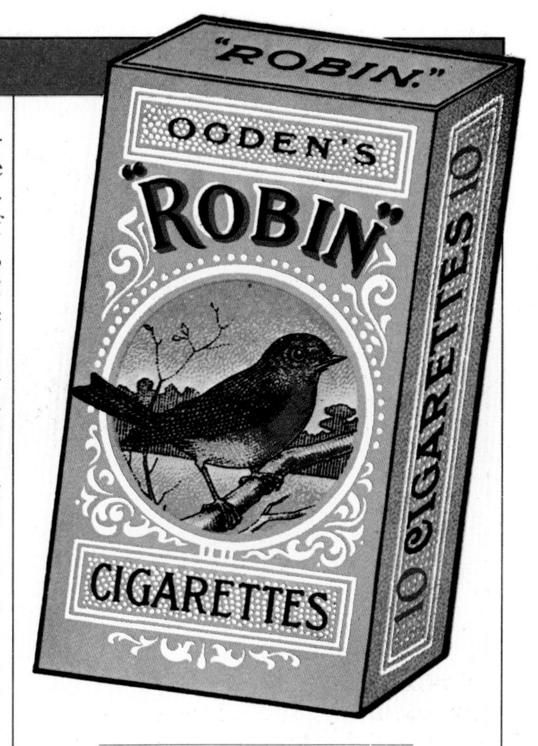


OGDEN'S ROBIN CIGARETTE CASE.

Advertising accounted for 1.1d per lb of sales in 1924; the high cost of these newer forms of advertising meant that in 1931 the figure had risen to over 3.5d and Wills alone spent more than £750,000 in that year. The older forms of advertising were gradually scaled down; obviously, many of the showcards and other forms of window dressing that had hitherto been distributed fairly indiscriminately were never used for their intended purpose and this was an aspect of advertising budgeting which needed revision. Hence, the big temporary displays and special promotions were limited to the larger outlets and the principal brands; money thus released was poured into press advertising, radio and film commercials, neon signs, wall paintings, sun blinds and other shop facia displays that would have a more direct impact on the man (and, increasingly, the woman) in the street.

The introduction of branding, the development of mass-production methods and the spending of a few hundred pounds a year on showcards and press advertising had, in the second half of the nineteenth century, represented a revolution in selling techniques. Now, in the brave new world of the twenties and thirties, another revolution was under way, and instead of the on-the-spot initiative of local retailers and the supreme skills of the chromolithographers, the road lay open for other, more modern forms of advertising and marketing: the radio or TV commercial and the gift scheme, the jingle and the selling slogan. Doubtless, in fifty year's time, a Player's No. 6 gift catalogue or an Embassy shop-window mobile will have the same nostalgic appeal that Hero, the Ogden's Coolie, Captain Capstan or the Wills' Fireflies have today; we can only wait and see ■

## PIPE DREAMS

Ogden's Tabs were introduced in 1900 to compete with Wills' Wild Woodbine and Cinderella brands in the 5 for 1d market. The launch was backed by attractive and extensive advertising, such as the showcard (opposite). Like many early pieces of promotional material, the image could easily have been relettered and used for a variety of products. Until the 1890s, the majority of advertisements had been purely typographical, as can be seen on the horse-drawn omnibus (below); only the metal sign for Player's Navy Cut carries an illustration.

OGDEN'S "TABS"
Cigarettes
OGDEN'S
"TAB"
ALBUM

Ever since the days of Sir Walter Raleigh, tobacco and Red Indians have been synonymous in the popular imagination; 'Cigar Store Injuns' can still occasionally be found today. The showcard (opposite) dates from 1924, that (below) from pre-World War I.

"WESTWARD HO!"

SMOKING MIXTURE

W. D. & H. O. WILLS, BRISTOL & LONDON.

# Pipe Dreams

Though *Hero* is the ship most closely associated with Player's tobacco (see pp. 32-3), other vessels have been commemorated on the famous sailor's cap ribbon, among them HMS *Invincible* and, as here, HMS *Excellent*. The show-card (opposite) appeared in 1946 and the Wren (below) is from the same era.

H.M.S. EXCELLENT
PLAYER'S
NAVY CUT
Player's
Please

## PIPE DREAMS

The Imperial Tobacco Company was formed in 1901 as a concerted defence by the British tobacco manufacturers against a threatened takeover by the American Tobacco Company; its aims are outlined in the press notice (below). A.T.C.'s products, such as Allen & Ginter's Richmond Gem, had previously been distributed in the U.K. by their agents who produced their own indigenous advertising (opposite). This showcard was found in Ogden's archives. A 'tobacco war' raged between the two giants for a year, at the end of which A.T.C. admitted defeat and sold Ogden's, the only major U.K. company they had been able to take control of, back into British hands. A.T.C. acquired a substantial minority interest on the board of I.T.C. and in future each group handled the other's export business in its own territories in a two-way trading agreement. The advertising of these products was undertaken by the distributors.

*To the*

# British Public

**Americans, whose markets are closed by prohibitive tariffs against British goods, have declared their intention of monopolising the Tobacco Trade of this Country.**

*It is for the* British Public to decide *whether* **BRITISH LABOUR, CAPITAL,** *and* **TRADE** *are to be* **subordinate** *to the American System of* Trust Monopoly *and* **all that is implied therein.**

THE

# Imperial Tobacco Co.

(Of Great Britain and Ireland) Limited.

About to be incorporated under the Companies Acts 1862 to 1900.

will be an AMALGAMATION of British Manufacturers who have closed their ranks with the determination to hold the BRITISH TRADE *for* BRITISH PEOPLE. Its aim is to provide the vast Smoking Public with CIGARETTES and TOBACCOS, unexcelled in quality, and made solely by means of **BRITISH Labour and Capital.**

THE VARIOUS BRANDS OF THE UNDERSIGNED MANUFACTURERS HAVE A REPUTATION FOR EXCELLENCE THE WORLD OVER.

The names of the Manufacturers forming THE IMPERIAL TOBACCO CO. are a guarantee that the products of their factories are **The Best** that a combination of **SKILL, JUDGMENT, and EXPERIENCE** can produce.

*W. D. & H. O. Wills, Ltd.* — Bristol.
*Edwards, Ringer & Bigg, Ltd.* — Bristol.
*Franklyn, Davey & Co.* — Bristol.

*Lambert & Butler, Ltd.* — London.
*Hignett's Tobacco Co., Ltd.* — London.
*Adkin & Sons* — London.

*John Player & Sons, Ltd.* — Nottingham.

*Hignett Bros. & Co., Ltd.* — Liverpool.
*William Clarke & Son, Ltd.* — Liverpool.
*Richmond Cavendish Co., Ltd.* — Liverpool.

*Stephen Mitchell & Son* — Glasgow.
*F. & J. Smith* — Glasgow.
*D. & J. Macdonald* — Glasgow.

RICHMOND GEM

CIGARETTES

ALLEN & GINTER,

HE AMERICAN TOBACCO Cº SUCCESSOR. U.S.

# Pipe Dreams

Pipe smoking has usually been depicted in advertising as a solitary solace, but here there is an emphasis on a spirit of sharing. It is regrettable that I.T.C.'s systematic numbering and cataloguing of advertising material dates only from 1905 since, in the showcard for Wills' Old Friend (opposite), the style of artwork, the workmen's clothes – note how the carpenter is a cut above the labourer in the matter of dress – and the condition of the card indicate a date possibly as early as 1890. The press advertisement for Player's Navy Mixture (below) can be dated much more accurately, however, for it is taken from the *Graphic* in June 1906.

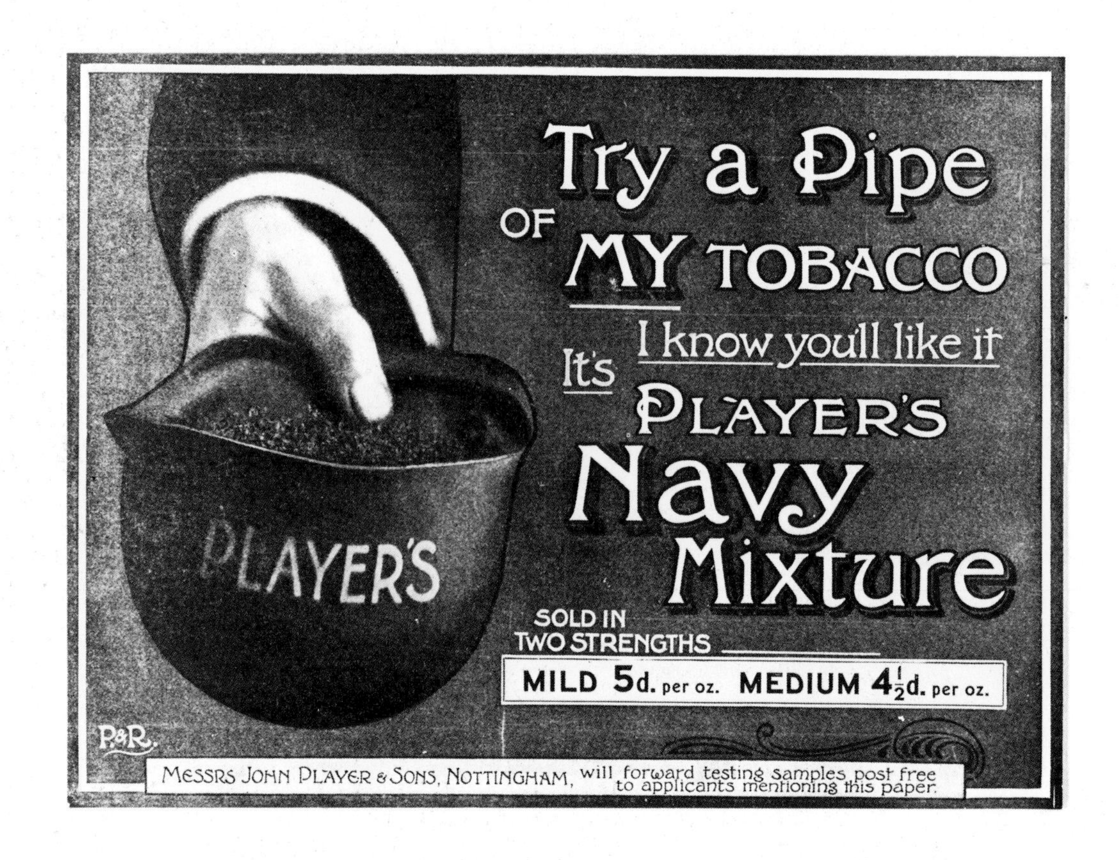

"Old Friend"

W. D. & H. O. Wills

TRADE MARK

Bristol

BARCLAY & FRY LONDON, E.C.

# PIPE DREAMS

Player's Weights, like the other penny cigarettes, were aimed essentially at the popular market, but the showcard of 1907 (opposite) sees them being smoked in much more exalted circles, where hand-made cigarettes would still be the norm. By 1930, when the Noel Coward figure (below) could be found lounging among the pages of the *Bystander*, machine-made cigarettes were being enjoyed right across the social spectrum.

5 FOR 1D. PLAYER'S 5 FOR 1D.

"WEIGHTS"

PLAYER'S

"WEIGHTS" CIGARETTES

MADE FROM PURE VIRGINIA TOBACCO.

PLAYER'S

"WEIGHTS" CIGARETT

E FROM PURE VIRGINIA

PLAYER'S

WEIGHTS

THE ORIGINAL

MADE FROM

PURE

VIRGINIA

TOBACCO

PLAYER'S

WEIGHTS

THE ORIGINAL

MADE FROM

PURE

VIRGINIA

TOBACCO

No 134

ISSUED BY THE IMPERIAL TOBACCO CO. (OF GREAT BRITAIN & IRELAND), LIMITED.

## PIPE DREAMS

Tobacco advertising in its infancy was far less stringently regulated that it is today when, among other considerations, the use of children and racial caricatures is expressly forbidden. The pre-1904 comic showcard for Ogden's Midnight Flake (opposite) is a good example of the association of visual images with brand names; the equally apposite and cheerful showcard (below) dates from the same era

I'm all right!

SMOKING
MIDNIGHT
FLAKE

OGDEN'S MIDNIGHT FLAKE

OGDEN'S.

# PIPE DREAMS

Two historic showcards: Cinderella and Wild Woodbine, introduced in 1888, were the first low-priced, machine-made cigarettes in the U.K. Despite minimal promotion, annual sales of the two brands in the 1890s were counted in hundreds of millions. For many years, cigarette smoking was virtually equated with Woodbines; even today, in some parts of Norfolk, cigarettes are still referred to colloquially as 'bines' (Tabs was another brand whose name entered common parlance to mean cigarettes in general). Wills adapted a painting supplied to them by a Bond Street gallery to produce a showcard for Cinderella (opposite), issued in 1898; the practice of making paintings into advertisements was quite common in Victorian times, the most famous example being the use of Millais' 'Bubbles' to promote Pear's Soap. The Woodbine showcard (below) is entirely typical of advertisements for this brand in the early 1900s, though this particular example was produced as late as 1924.

"CINDERELLA"
CIGARETTES.

1d. PER PACKET OF 5.

W. D. & H. O. WILLS Ltd.

## PIPE DREAMS

The joys and pitfalls of motoring have given scope for many advertising images over the years. The great Tom Browne produced the lighthearted showcard (opposite) for Weights in 1909; possibly it might originally have been intended as an advertisement for one of Player's pipe tobaccos, since the unhurried carter is clearly enjoying a clay. The press advertisement for Gold Flake (below) was used in the 1930s; note the licence plate.

MADE ENTIRELY OF VIRGINIA TOBACCO

"YOU might just pull up at the first tobacconist's. I want some Gold Flake."

*Wills's*

GOLD FLAKE

CIGARETTES

10 *for* 6d

*W. D. & H. O. Wills, Branch of The Imperial Tobacco Co. (of Great Britain & Ireland), Ltd.*

PLAYER'S
"WEIGHTS"

TOM BROWNE

XYZO

CIGARETTES 5 FOR 1D.

"NONE SO DEAF
AS THOSE WHO
WON'T HEAR."

No 523

# PIPE DREAMS

Ogden's produced probably the most inventive and certainly the most colourful point-of-sale material of all the I.T.C. constituents in the years before World War I. The die-cut show-card for Coolie tobacco (opposite) could be seen in shop windows in 1913. Not for them were the endless re-workings of the sailor theme popular with Player's and Wills (below), though this curiously bug-eyed specimen represents one of the few occasions on which Gold Flake was advertised in this way.

OGDEN'S
"COOLIE" CUT PLUG
Ogden's
"COOLIE"
CUT 3½d. PLUG
PER OZ.

## PIPE DREAMS

The small showcard (opposite) is a beautiful turn-of-the-century period piece from Wills; note the archaic spelling. Though the abolition of slavery had ended the worst abuses of the tobacco plantation system, conditions generally were still not quite as idyllic as this image might suggest. The Virginia landscape had not greatly changed since Sir Walter Raleigh (below, in a poster of 1920 by Septimus E. Scott) first gazed over it.

# PIPE DREAMS

John Player safeguarded his control over the pre-packed tobacco which he began selling in 1877 by introducing his first trade mark, a drawing of Nottingham Castle which is still known today. More familiar, however, is another Player's trade mark – the famous sailor's head. It took shape gradually; first in 1883 with the head and shoulders alone, and then in 1888 with the lifebuoy frame lettered 'Player's Navy Cut'. In 1891 two ships were added: HMS *Britannia*, a wooden three-decker with 120 guns, and (always to the right of the sailor) the much more modern cruiser HMS *Hero*, built in 1885. The latter gave her name to the sailor's cap band, but owing to an oversight the letters HMS were omitted and the sailor was drawn with two, instead of the correct three, white stripes on his collar. The design was registered in 1891 with these inaccuracies unspotted; on legal advice, they have never been corrected. Hero appeared in various guises: bearded and clean-shaven, young and old, looking to left and right, even (as on p. 96) seen from behind. In 1927 his image was standardised on all packaging, advertising and display material using a design based on a painting by A. D. McCormick (opposite) which was originally produced in 1905 and is still in use today.

SMOKE PLAYER'S NAVY CUT, beautifully Cool and Sweet Smoking. Ask at all Tobacco Sellers, Stores, &c., and take no other than "PLAYER'S NAVY CUT." Sold ONLY in 1 oz. Packets, 2 oz. Boxes, and 4 oz. Tins, which keep the Tobacco always in fine smoking condition. The genuine bears the Trade Mark, "NOTTINGHAM CASTLE," on every Packet and Tin. Player's Navy Cut CIGARETTES can now be obtained of all leading Tobacconists, Stores, &c., in Packets containing 12.

PLAYER'S
HERO
NAVY CUT
No 3017A
REGD No 154011.

Ogden's claim in the showcard of 1890 (opposite) that Guinea Gold had the 'Largest Sale in the World' was completely unsubstantiated, but then Victorian advertisers never let truth stand in the way of a good copy line. Though the brand, selling at 10 for 3d, was certainly a big seller in its day, it was the introduction in 1900 of Tabs, at 5 for 1d, which put the Liverpool company firmly on the map. Richmond Gem (below) was another of their popular brands; it was distributed by them on behalf of Allen & Ginter, the second largest tobacco manufacturer in the U.S.A. and a major constituent of the American Tobacco Company.

RICHMOND GEM

CIGARETTES.
UNEQUALLED
FOR DELICACY AND FLAVOR.

OGDEN'S "Guinea" Gold Cigarettes

OGDEN'S GUINEA GOLD

OGDEN'S "GUINEA" GOLD CIGARETTES

Largest Sale in the World.

# PIPE DREAMS

Though the figures and selling slogans used in tobacco advertising tended to be fairly permanent institutions, there was always scope for one-off, short-term opportunism. Wills cashed in on the excitement engendered by the gold rush of 1898 with this contemporary showcard for Capstan (opposite). Note the mis-spelling of Klondike; such vagaries are not uncommon in nineteenth-century advertising. Typical of press advertising in this period, with its concentration on simple information rather than entertainment, is the example (below), which appeared in a Christmas 1894 copy of the *Pall Mall Budget*.

"WILLS'S"

# NAVY CUT

"CAPSTAN" BRAND.

Can now be obtained in 2 oz. Patent Air-Tight Tins

IN THREE GRADES OF STRENGTH, VIZ.:

**" MILD," Yellow Label.**
**" MEDIUM," Blue Label.**
**" FULL," Chocolate Label.**

As well as in 1 oz. Packets and ¼ lb. Patent Air-Tight Tins, by all dealers in Tobacco.

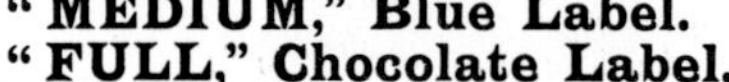

**W. D. & H. O. WILLS, LD.**

**BRISTOL AND LONDON.**

THE ONLY COMFORT IN KLONDYKE

See these nuggets?
I'd give the lot for another tin of
WILLS'S "CAPSTAN"

# PIPE DREAMS

Most of the U.K. tobacco industry's advertising material was prepared and printed by Mardon's of Bristol. Outside artists were commissioned for the illustrations, and the lettering was added by artists working in-house. Though their work has often gone unrecognised, the latter were often highly talented. The Honey Dew showcard (opposite) dates from 1902; the image (below) gives a somewhat unfortunate impression of country life in the fields of France between 1914 and 1918.

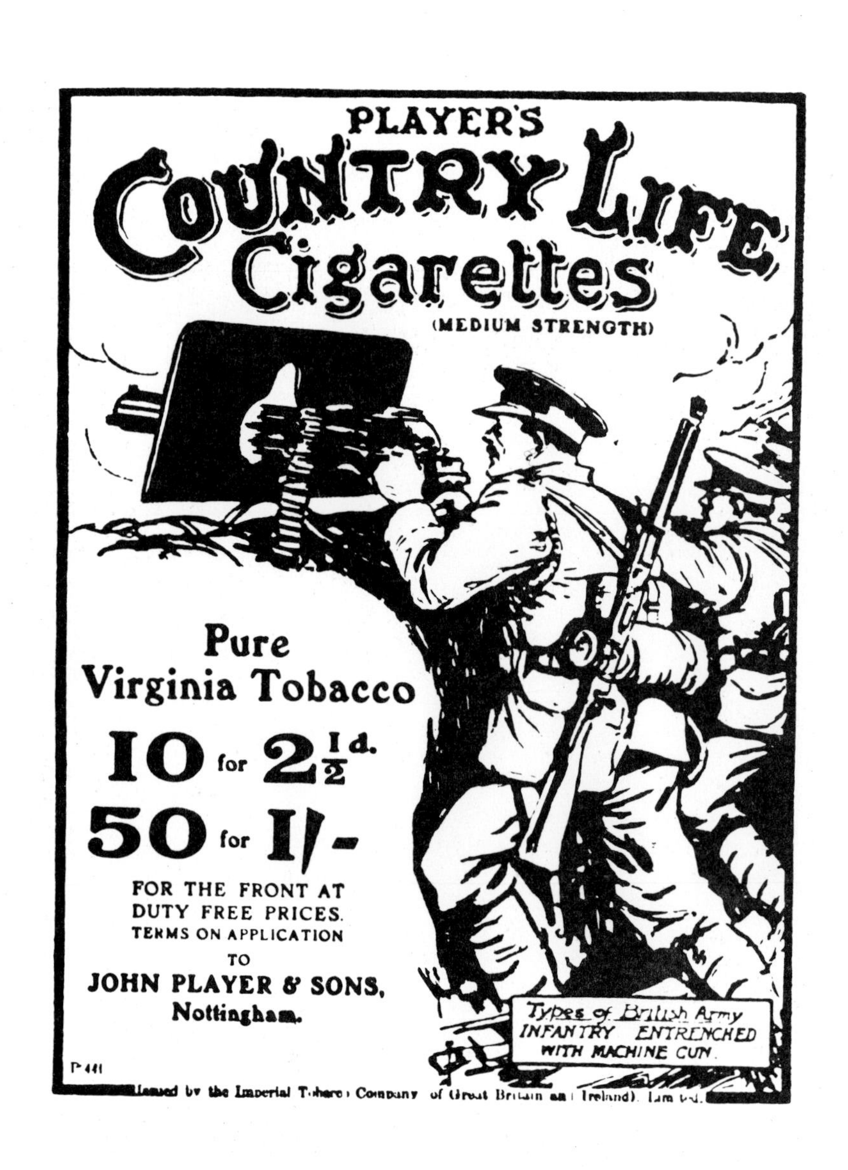

PLAYER'S
HONEY-DEW

# PIPE DREAMS

War offered a heaven-sent opportunity for tobacco manufacturers to produce advertising which would both increase sales and express appropriately patriotic sentiments: (below) an advertisement for Ogden's Guinea Gold placed in an edition of the *Graphic* after the end of the Boer War and (opposite) a punning showcard of 1915. The length of the funnels has been exaggerated to emphasise the point.

"WILD WOODBINE"
CIGARETTES.
In the Dardanelles.
The five-funnelled Russian Cruiser "ASKOLD",
commonly known as "The packet of Woodbines.
W. D. & H. O. WILLS, BRISTOL & LONDON.

Player's Navy Mixture almost invariably made use of a sailor figure in advertising. The example (opposite) is the work of T. Friedenson and gives a good idea of the type of packaging Player's were using for this brand in 1916. The showcard (below) is from about eight years earlier.

# PLAYER'S

IN
THREE
STRENGTHS

MILD,
MEDIUM
AND
WHITE
LABEL.

# NAVY MIXTURE

ISSUED BY THE IMPERIAL TOBACCO CO. (OF GREAT BRITAIN & IRELAND) LIMITED.

## PIPE DREAMS

Historical scenes were a great favourite with I.T.C. The showcard (opposite) is the work of G. E. Shepheard; it was issued in 1906. Though a pipe and a pint (or whatever your favourite tipple might be) have always been a popular combination and figure regularly in brewer's advertisements, surprisingly little promotional material for tobacco shows the two being enjoyed together. Much more common was Elizabethan imagery, such as the 1920s showcard reproduced (below).

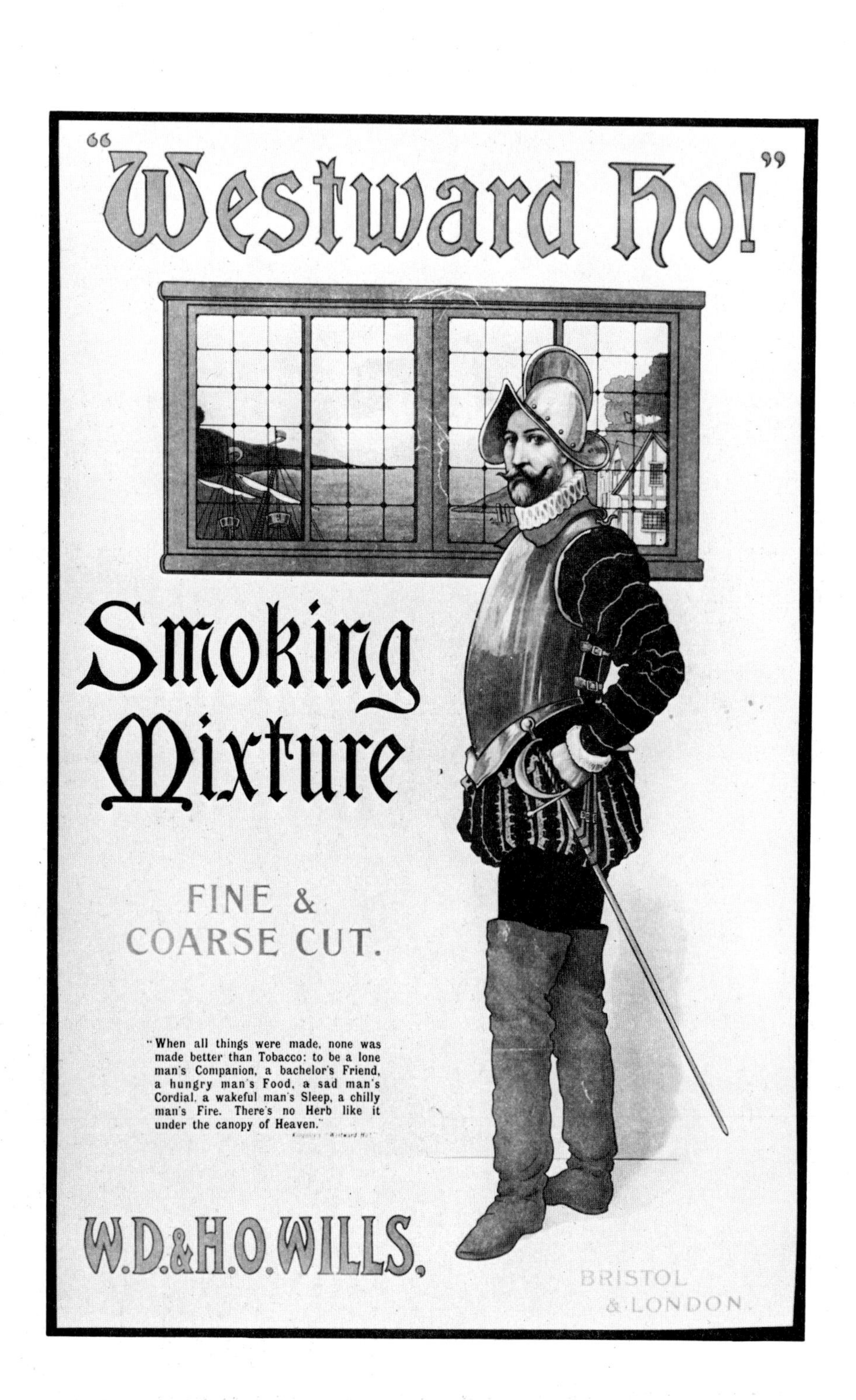

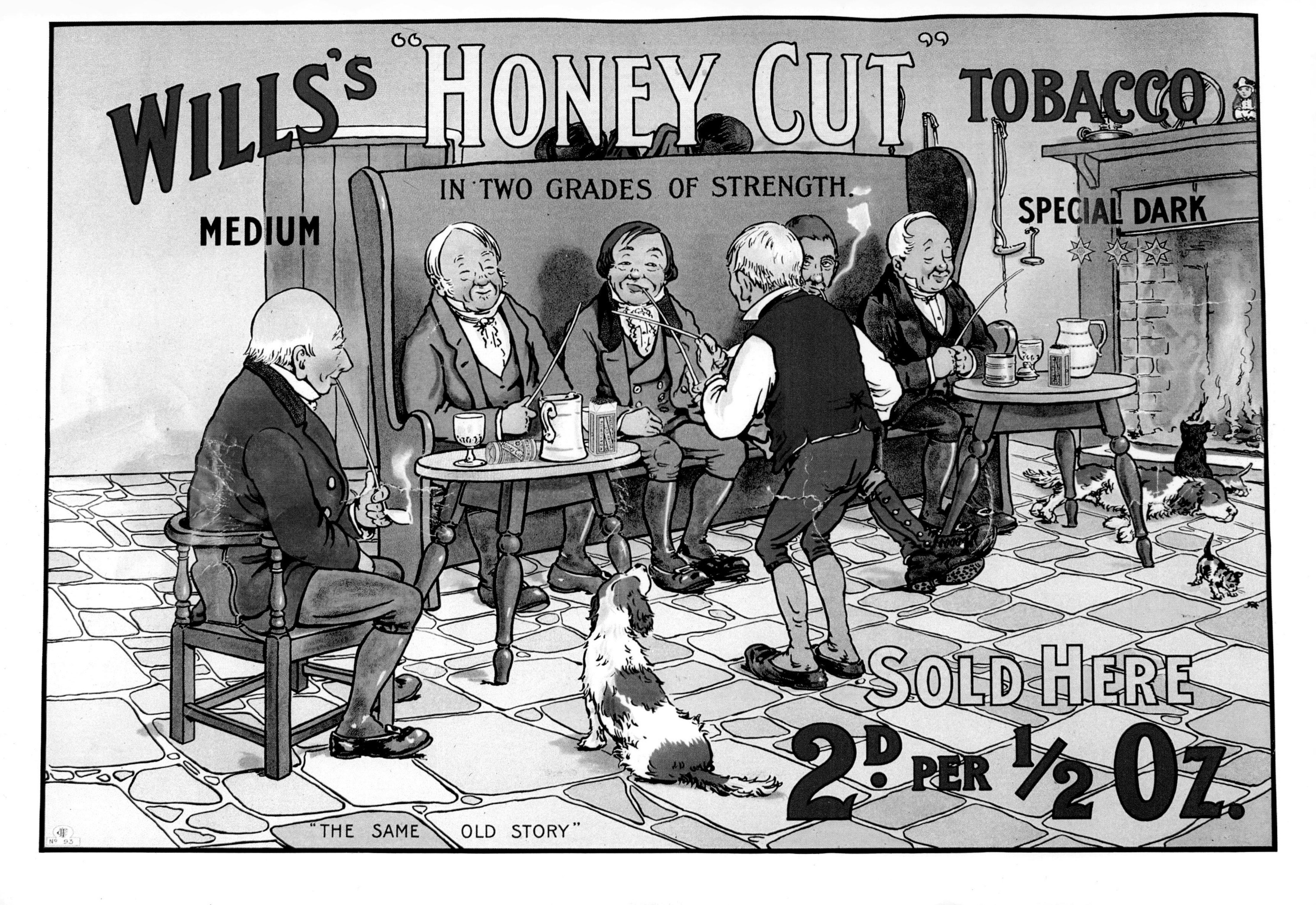
WILLS's "HONEY CUT" TOBACCO
IN TWO GRADES OF STRENGTH.
MEDIUM
SPECIAL DARK
SOLD HERE
2D. PER 1/2 OZ.
"THE SAME OLD STORY"
No 93

# PIPE DREAMS

The famous slogan 'Player's Please' began to take shape in 1924, initially as 'Player's Will Please You' and later as 'They're Player's and They Please'. In its familiar abbreviated form the phrase first appeared in block lettering until George Green, the company's first advertising manager, put it into script in his own immaculate hand. It was used as it stood, coming into general use in 1927. The 1931 style (opposite) has it in a light letter, others have it shaded, while the example (below), taken from the *London Magazine* in 1929, sees it appearing in bold.

Player's
Please

## PIPE DREAMS

Two excellent showcards for Ogden's St Julien tobacco. Unlike their I.T.C. colleagues Player's and Wills, the Liverpool firm made little use of seafaring imagery and such work as they did produce in this vein often had a pleasingly original angle, such as the example (opposite) which dates from c. 1910-11. The cut-out (below) was produced by Ogden's in 1908.

SMOKE

# St JULIEN

TOBACCO

Cool & Fragrant.

# PIPE DREAMS

The interior of a tobacconist's shop (opposite) as seen in a Wills showcard of 1900. Note the showcards on display, the tobacco packets and the scales used for weighing out loose tobacco. The photograph (below), of slightly later date, shows the exterior of a hairdresser's premises which doubled as a tobacconist's – a common practice, since both attracted large numbers of male customers. The painted advertisements on the wall, the showcards in the window and the enamel signs below the sills will be noted; these were the staples of high-street advertising at the time.

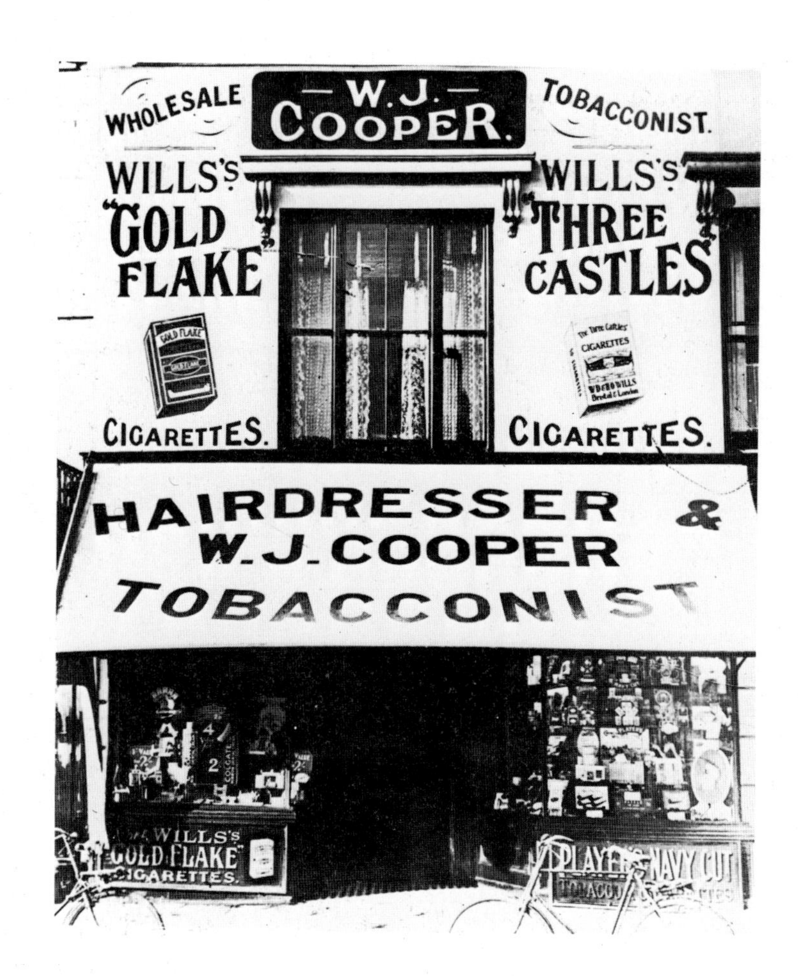

WILL'S
SUPERFINE SHAGG
W.D.& H.O.WILLS
WILL'S
Superfine
SHAGG
·W·D & H·O·WILLS·L.TD
·BRISTOL & LONDON·

# Pipe Dreams

Christmas was always a good time for special promotions, and the seasonal showcard (opposite) was issued by Player's in 1933. In the lean days of the early 1930s such cheerful advertising was doubly welcome; (below) is a sample of magazine and newspaper advertisements placed by Wills in various publications the previous year.

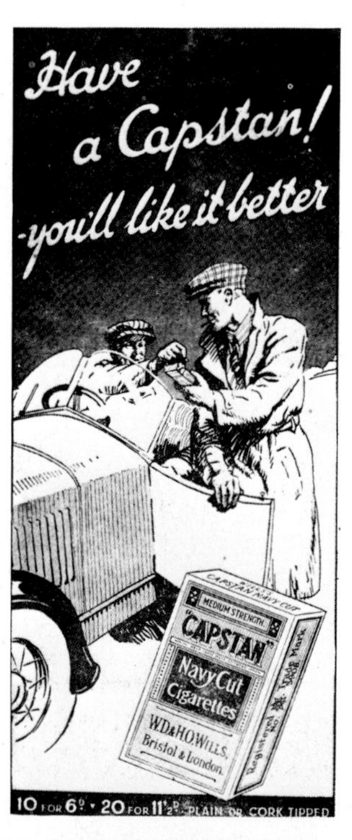

Player's Please
EXCELLENT
CIGARETTES "MEDIUM" 50

# PIPE DREAMS

The contrasting leisure habits of half a century show through in these two showcards: the brisk, bracing image of the Edwardian seaside holiday (opposite), the go-as-you-please casualness of the post-austerity years (below).

PLEASED TO SEE YOU SMOKE

"Tabs"

Cigarettes.

Apart from the lettering, neither of these showcards (that opposite from 1919, below dated 1916) bears any relation to tobacco. Both demonstrate the timeless appeal of a pretty face, particularly since the tobacco market at that time was still almost exclusively dominated by males.

"WILD WOODBINE"
HARRY WOOLLEY
CIGARETTES.
W.D. & H.O. WILLS, Bristol & London.

## PIPE DREAMS

Smoking among women became voguish in the 1920s; before then, any woman bold enough to smoke in public would have been considered more than a little 'fast'. In earlier years many advertisements had stressed the strength or masculine associations of tobacco; with the arrival of the 'new woman' I.T.C.'s advertising agents were instructed to soften their material up to make them appeal to the increasing numbers of women buyers. By 1929, women alone were smoking almost as many cigarettes as had been annually consumed in all markets thirty years previously. Both men and women appear in Tom Browne's typically jovial showcard of 1923 for Player's Weights (opposite), while the cut-out (below) sees an emancipated girl smoking on her own – though the image could have been linked to a more appropriate brand. Perhaps Wills' motives were subtle.

PLAYER'S "WEIGHTS" Cigarettes

PLAYER'S
"WEIGHTS"
CIGARETTES

"HELD UP"

in packets of 5,
and card boxes of 100.

XY 20

TOM BROWNE

# PIPE DREAMS

Though the increase in women smokers had a noticeable effect on the advertising of many brands of cigarettes, pipe tobaccos and the stronger cigarettes retained their masculine associations. Forty years separate these two advertisements for Capstan, but the bias and family likeness is clear.

# "CAPSTAN" NAVY CUT.

H.M.S. EXCELLENT

W.D. & H.O. WILLS + BRISTOL & LONDON +

TOBACCO & CIGARETTES

In Three grades of Strength

MILD, YELLOW LABEL

MEDIUM, BLUE ,,

FULL, CHOCOLATE ,,

H.M.S. EXCELLENT

W.D. & H.O. WILLS + BRISTOL & LONDON +

"LEST WE FORGET!"

ISSUED BY THE IMPERIAL TOBACCO CO. (OF GREAT BRITAIN & IRELAND), LIMITED.

The world of Pickwick and Jorrocks was often recalled in tobacco advertising, particularly for such a brand name as Country Life: (opposite) a blissful smoke, bees humming drowsily, dog dozing in the afternoon sun, jug of ale at hand – the work of H. M. Brock, 1907; (below) Cecil Aldin in his element with a 1912 showcard.

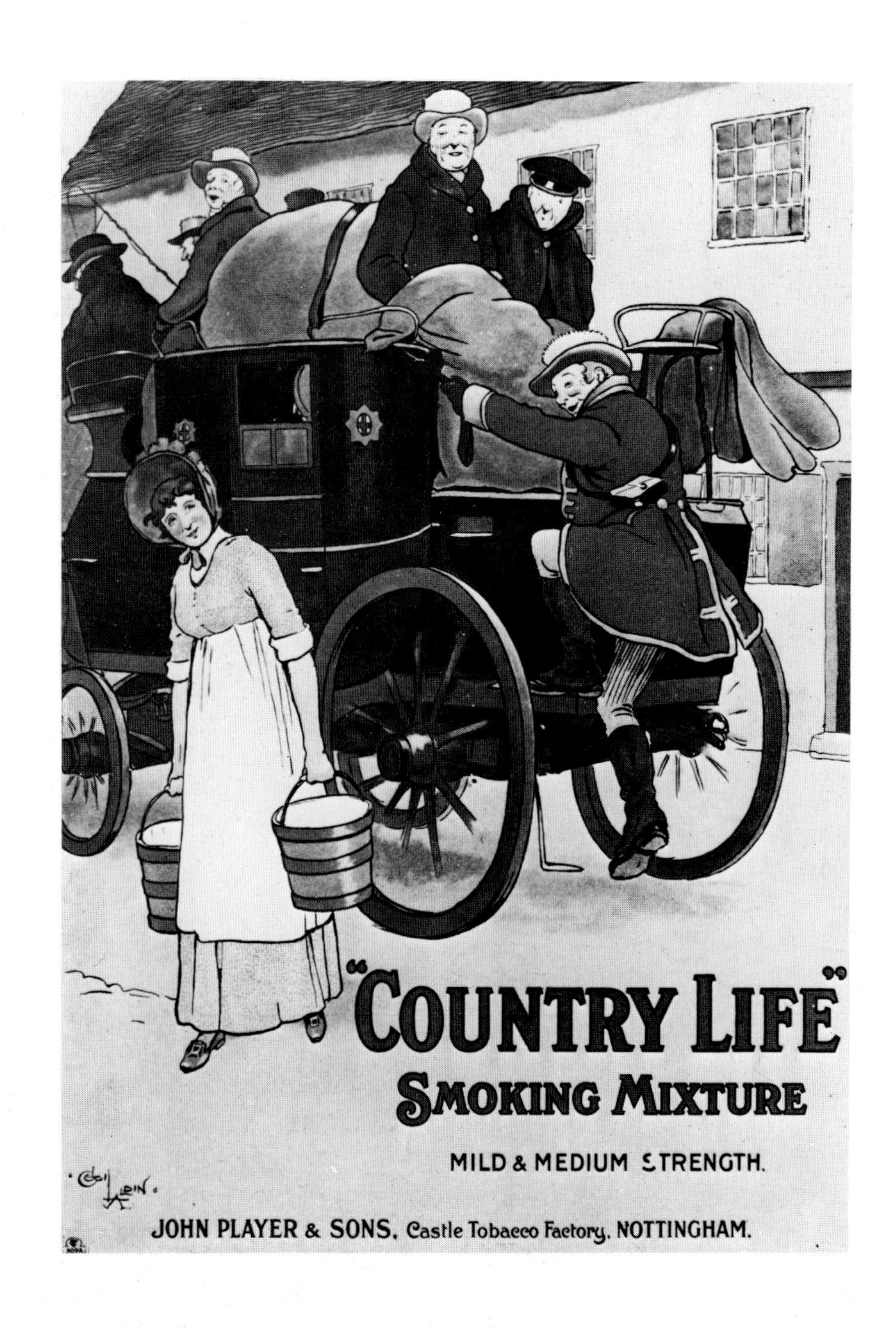

H·M·BROCK
Player's
"Country Life" Smoking Mixture
No 246
Issued by the Imperial Tobacco Co. (of Great Britain & Ireland) Ltd

## PIPE DREAMS

These two showcards with military themes form an interesting break from the more conventional nautical flavour of tobacco advertising. The example (opposite) is from c. 1907 and is the work of F. C. Wheeler; that (below) is by C. Clark of Tom Browne & Co. and is dated 1917. Though not perhaps as well known as the Red Indian or blackamoor figures, the Highlander is one of the traditional symbols of the tobacco trade. Its origins are said to go back to the eighteenth century, when a wooden statue of a Highlander used to stand outside the London shop of a tobacconist called David Wishart. Jacobite conspirators met here until the collapse of the 1745 Rebellion caused them to flee, leaving the lonely Highlander as a symbol of their lost cause and, in time, of the tobacco and snuff merchant.

"REDBREAST"
Flake
3D.
PER OZ.
F. C. Wheeler
No 192

A selection of nineteenth and early twentieth century tobacco and cigarette packaging. These rank among the most elaborately decorative examples of the early wrappings of branded goods; designs like these are still used for some long-established brands today.

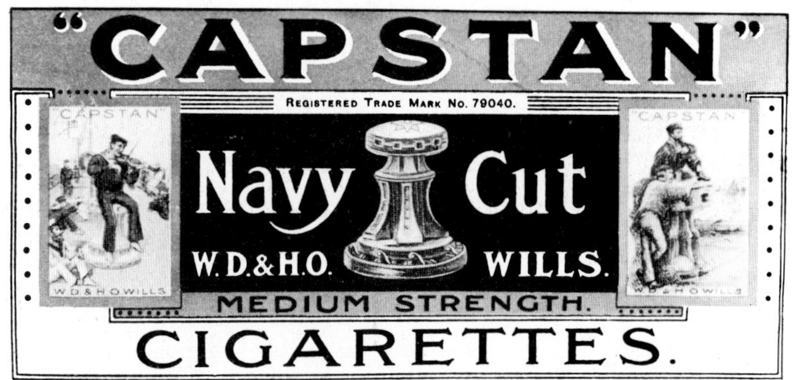

In 1oz & 2oz. Boxes & 4 oz. Air Tight Tins
"Capstan"
Navy Cut
Mild Yellow Label
Medium Strength Blue
Full Chocolate
W.D. & H.O. Wills.

Evening Star
Cigarettes
W.D. & H.O. Wills

"Old Times"
W.D. & H.O. Wills

Cigarettes "Sahara"
W.D. & H.O. Wills. Bristol & London

"Bulwark" Flake
W.D. & H.O. Wills.

"Heartsease" Bird's Eye
W.D. & H.O. Wills

"Autumn Gold"
Tobacco
W.D. & H.O. Wills
Bristol & London
Prize Medal
Trade Mark
Prize Medal

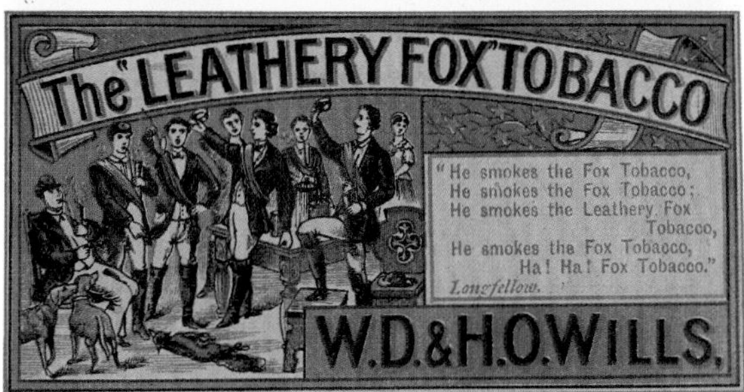
The "Leathery Fox" Tobacco
"He smokes the Fox Tobacco,
He smokes the Fox Tobacco;
He smokes the Leathery Fox Tobacco,
He smokes the Fox Tobacco,
Ha! Ha! Fox Tobacco."
Longfellow.
W.D. & H.O. Wills.

# PIPE DREAMS

The extraordinarily beautiful and erotic showcard for Player's Navy Cut (opposite) was issued in 1898. It is signed by V. Coray, one of the artists who worked for Tom Browne's design and lithography company in Nottingham, and stands in marked contrast to the cheery humour which is normally associated with their work. The sailor on the cut-out showcard (below) has the correct three stripes on his collar; Hero, due to an oversight, was copyrighted in 1891 with only two.

The ocean swell and scudding rain-clouds don't prevent the salty character (opposite) from enjoying a pipe of Wills' Bulwark tobacco. This showcard was produced in 1925; the Bulwark label (below) is a few years older than this.

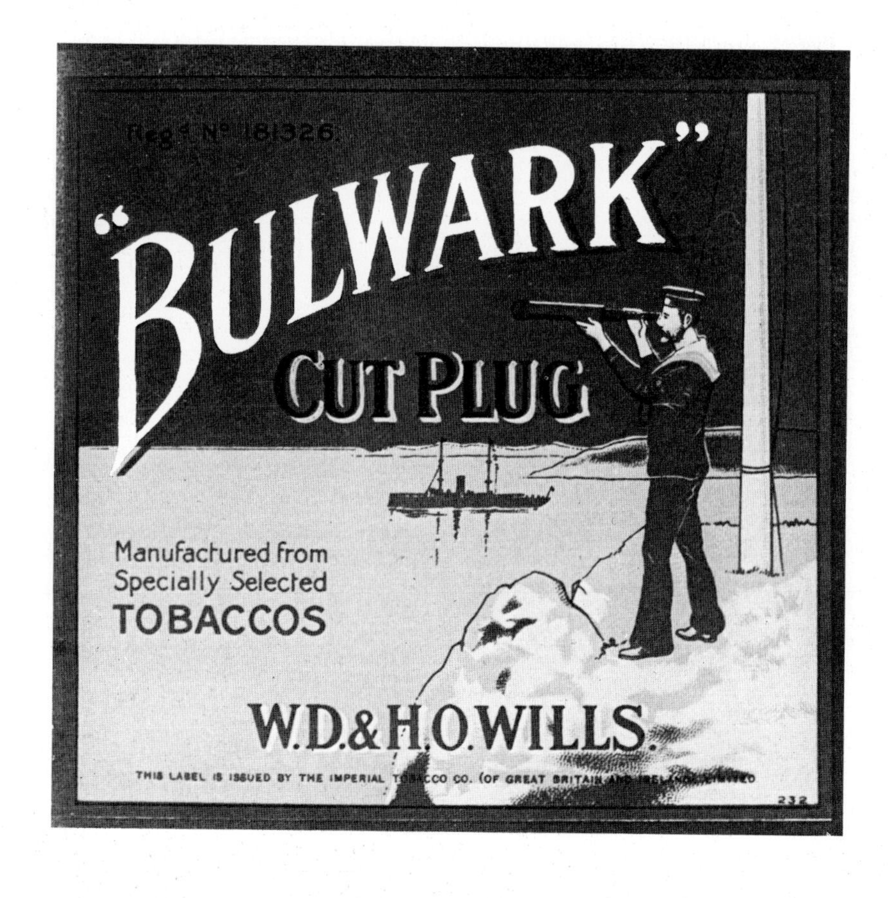

WILLS's "BULWARK"
CUT PLUG TOBACCO
W.D. & H.O. WILLS

# PIPE DREAMS

Evidently fairways were sufficiently uncongested in 1927 for the two golfers (opposite) to take time off their game for a smoke in the rough. Male camaraderie was also the theme of advertisements for Wills' Gold Flake published in newspapers in 1937, from which the silhouette drawings (below) have been taken.

PLAYER'S NAVY CUT
TOBACCO & CIGARETTES

4898

The early years saw some pretty bizarre advertisements being produced, but none more so than the showcard of 1904 (opposite). Almost as absurd (below) were showcards for Wills' Best Bird's Eye (1893) and Ogden's Robin (1931) and the choice of the brand name Parrot for one of Wills' blends – other curious brand names used by Wills included Leathery Fox, Nec Plus Ultra and Gossips.

SMOKE

"FIREFLY"

OBLIGE ME
WITH A LIGHT.

CIGARETTES

W. D. & H. O. WILLS,
BRISTOL & LONDON. ENGLAND.

In the inter-war period the number of magazines carrying colour advertising increased dramatically, and this medium was used to promote several top I.T.C. brands. Capstan was advertised (opposite) in a 1931 issue of the *Bystander*. The painting (below) by Bradshaw Crandell was intended for Canadian magazines in 1942 but in the event was never used for its original purpose.

MEDIUM STRENGTH
"CAPSTAN"
REGD TRADE MARK No 79040
Navy Cut
Cigarettes
W.D.&H.O.WILLS.
Bristol & London.
10 CIGARETTES
PUSH

# PIPE DREAMS

The illustrations (opposite) show some of the very first coloured cigarette cards, issued by Wills between 1888 and 1893. They were used to stiffen up the paper packets of cigarettes and reproduced not only contemporary packaging designs but also current posters and showcards. Over the years an extraordinary range of subjects were depicted on cigarette cards – indeed, it is difficult to think of a topic which wasn't, at one time or another, made into a series of cards. One set (below) even looked to the future for inspiration; issued by Stephen Mitchell & Son of Glasgow, a branch of I.T.C. whose most substantial sales were made north of the border, the cards were largely based on stills from Alexander Korda's 1936 science fiction film *Things To Come*, which was scripted by H. G. Wells.

GIANT TELESCOPE

GYRO-MOTOR RACE

SPACE-GUN

STREAM-LINED SPEED-SHIP

ANTI-GAS ARMOUR

LAUNCHING A SPACE-SHIP

TELEVISION

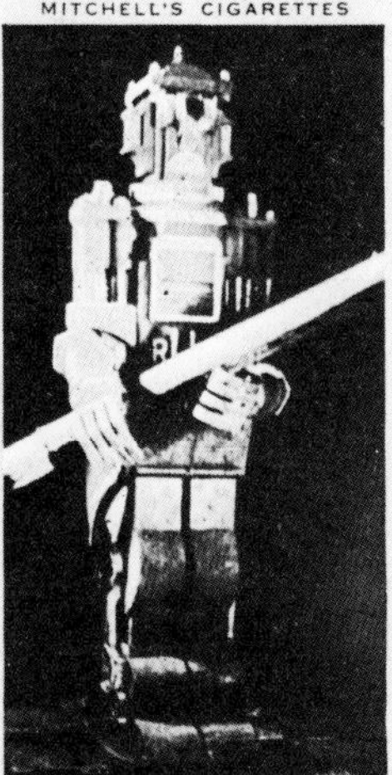


ROBOT OR MECHANICAL MAN

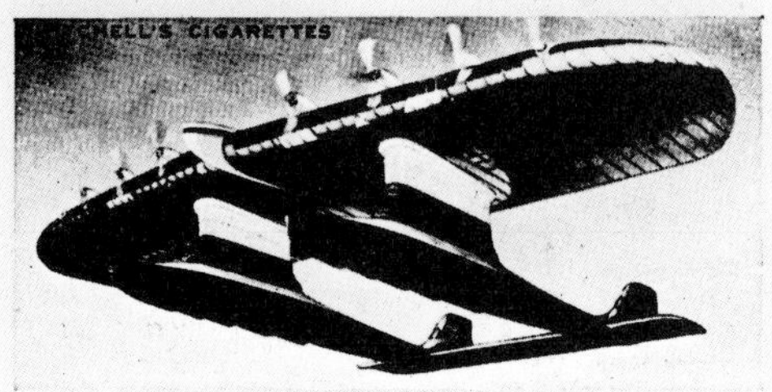


SUPER-AIRPLANE

RAILPLANE

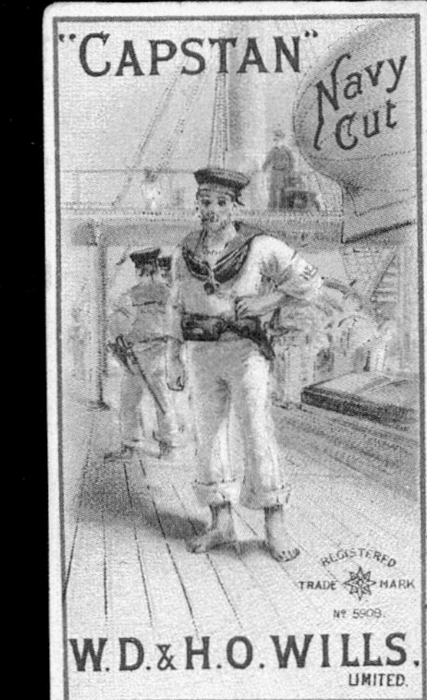

Wills's "Gold Flake"
W.D.&H.O.WILLS.
LIMITED.

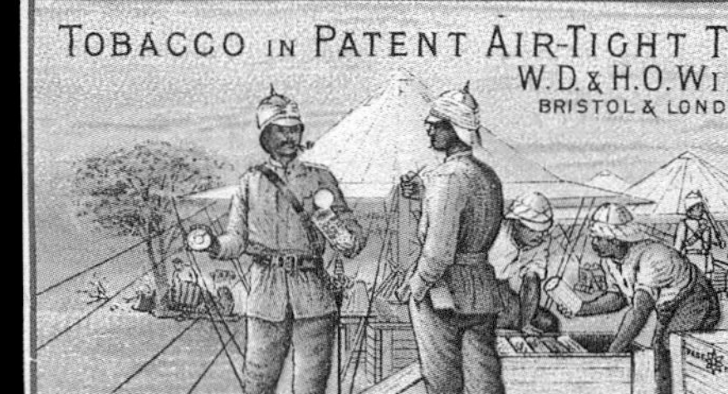

"Three Castles" Cigarettes
W.D.&H.O.Wills.

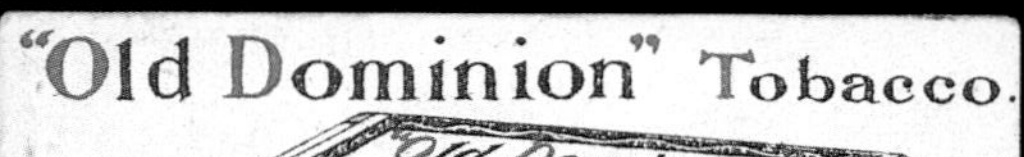


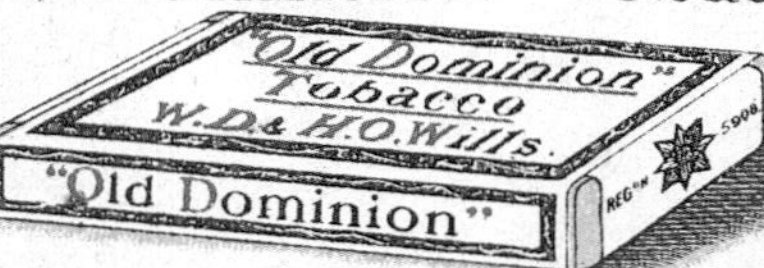


A mild coarse cut Tobacco suitable for Pipe or Cigarette.
In $\frac{1}{16}$ Square and $\frac{1}{8}$ Square Foil Packets, and $\frac{1}{4}$-lb Patent Tins.
W. D. & H. O. WILLS, LIMITED.

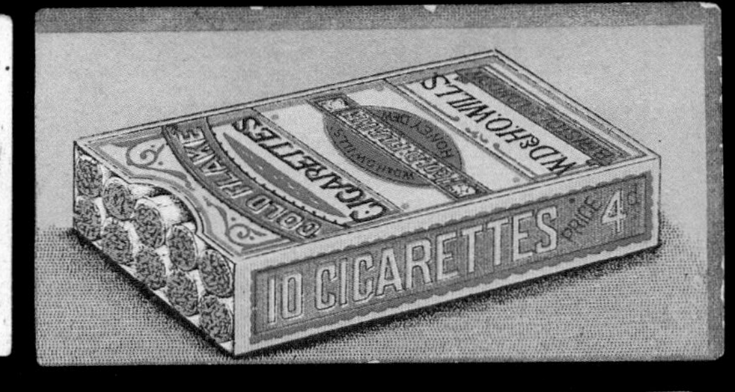


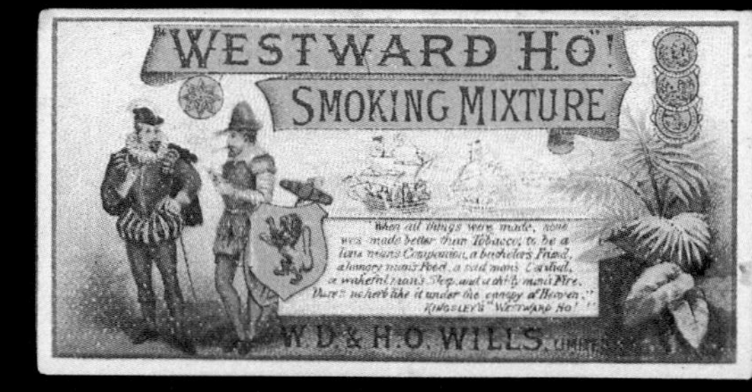


"GOLD FLAKE"

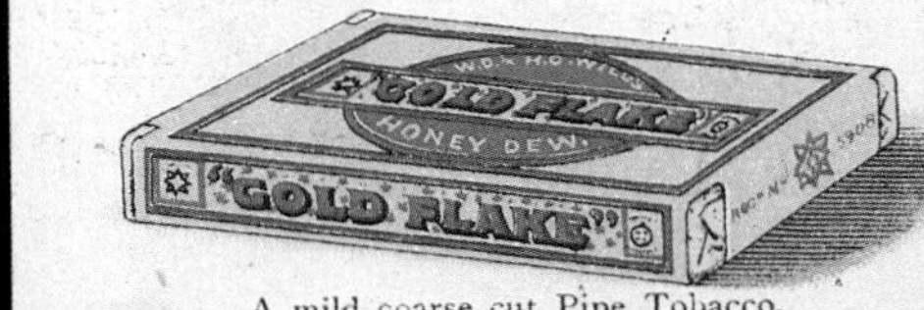

A mild coarse cut Pipe Tobacco.
W. D. & H. O. WILLS, LIMITED.

The "Three Castles" Tobacco.

Supplied in two grades of strength.
MILD—
FINE CUT, GREEN LABEL,
MEDIUM—
COARSE CUT, YELLOW LABEL
W.D.& H.O.WILLS.
LIMITED.

## PIPE DREAMS

Only a minority of early pictorial advertisements actually showed the product concerned, and then usually superimposed over the artwork or lettering. Most relied on the power of indirect association in the form of an interplay between the verbal and visual messages; puns were very popular (below). The Victorian and Edwardian public, who on the whole knew a good deal more about the flora and fauna around them than the average person does today, could readily make the connection between the cigarette and the wild flower from which it took its name in the showcards (opposite) – one by Victor Venner, from 1905, the other, dated 1907, by Alice Martineau, one of the very few women artists whose work was used in early tobacco advertising.

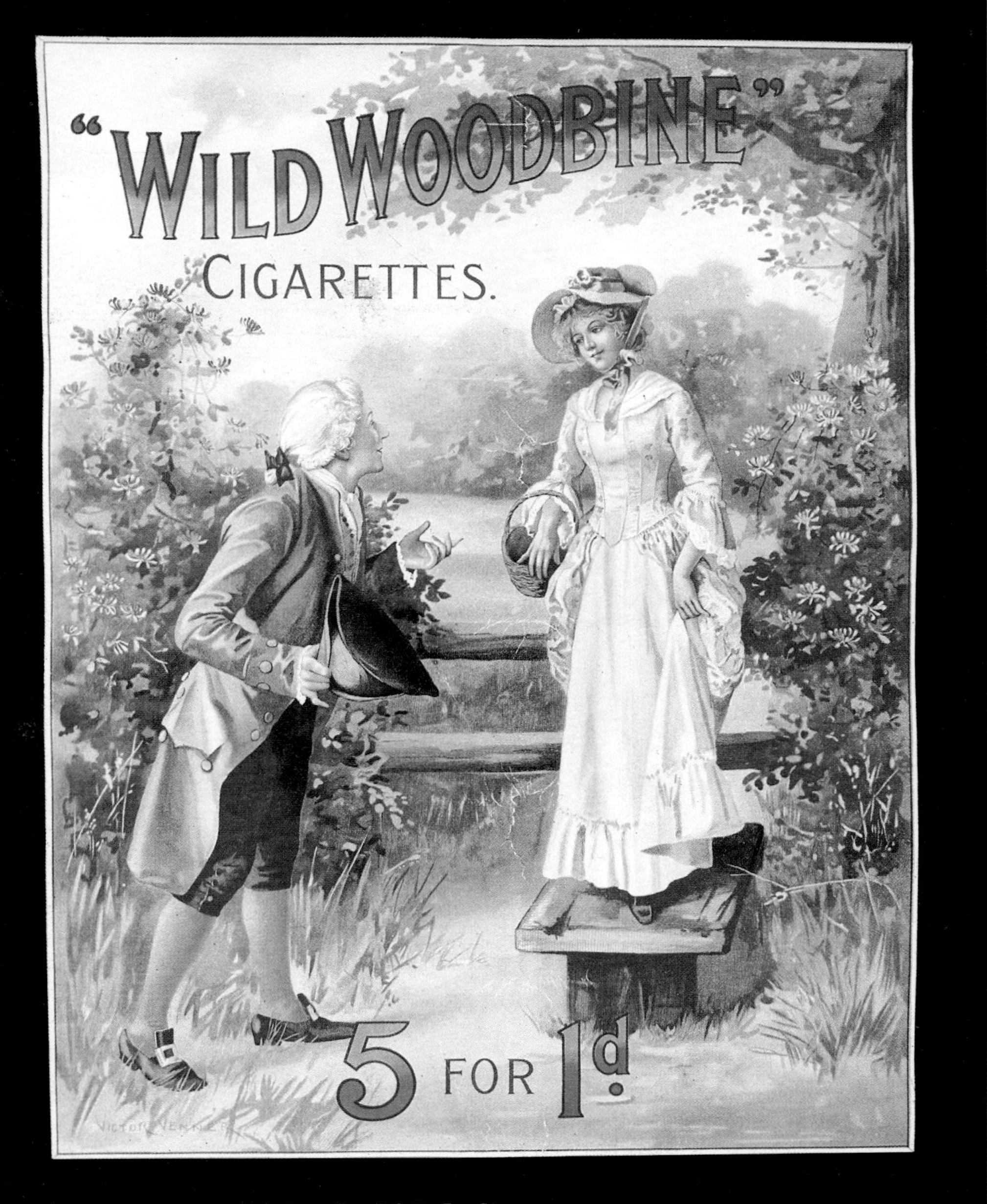
"WILD WOODBINE"
CIGARETTES.
5 FOR 1d.
W. D. & H. O. WILLS. BRISTOL & LONDON.

"WILD WOODBINE"
CIGARETTES.
FIVE FOR 1D.
W. D. & H. O. WILLS,
BRISTOL & LONDON.

# PIPE DREAMS

During World War I there was a large influx of Australian soldiers into Britain, which led to the adoption of the trade name Digger for the new blend of Empire-grown tobaccos introduced in 1917. Even as late as 1932, advertising of Digger retained strongly jingoistic sentiments (opposite). The showcard (below) dates from 1940.

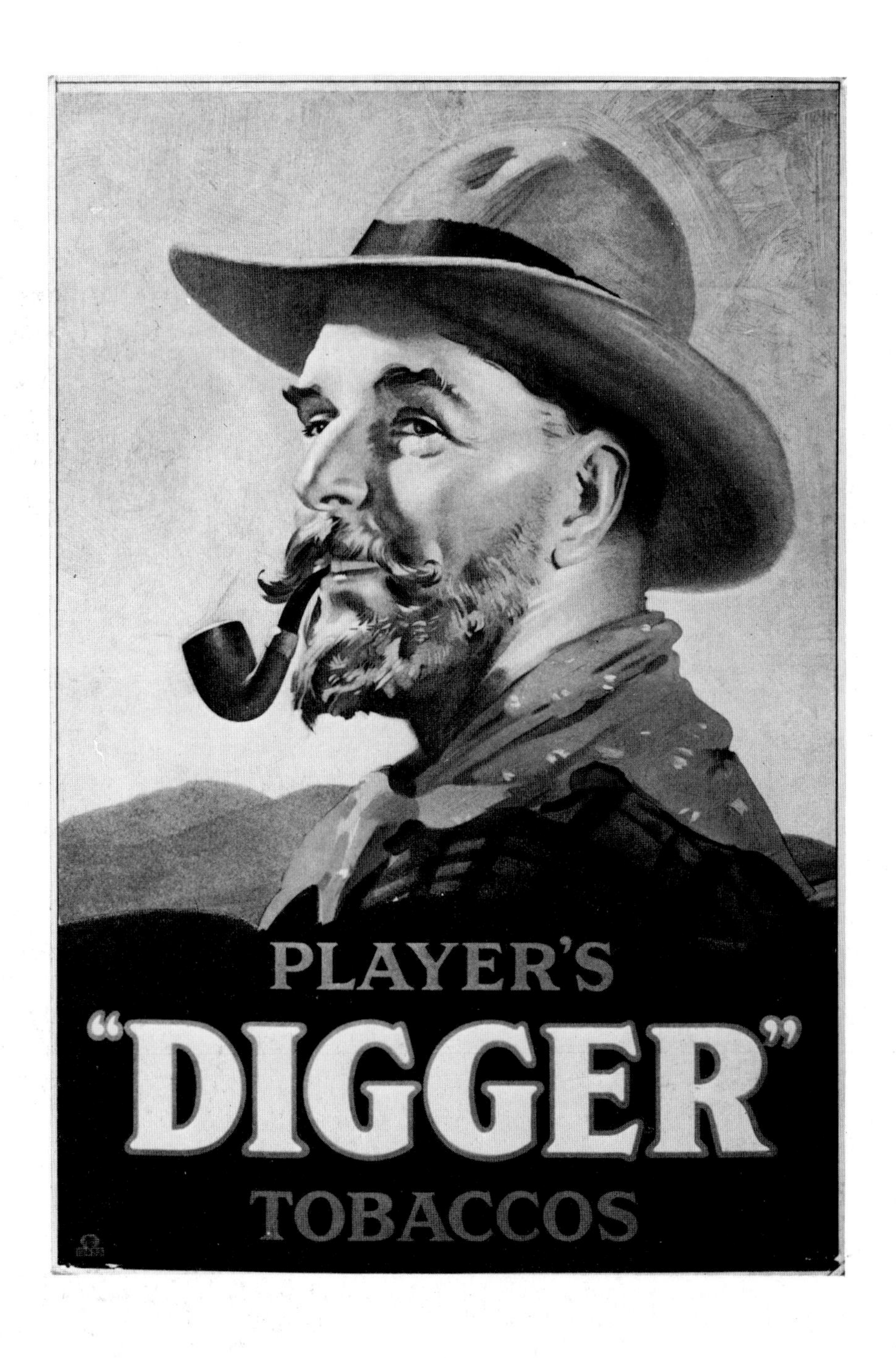

SUPPORT THE EMPIRE!
Smoke
PLAYER'S
"DIGGER"
8D.
PER OZ.

Advertising has frequently attempted to associate tobacco with sport and other healthy outdoor activities. The 1927 showcard (opposite) and a contemporary advertisement from the *Cricketer Annual* (below) are typical of this particular approach.

# PLAYER'S

Tobacco
& Cigarettes

ISSUED BY THE IMPERIAL TOBACCO CO. (OF GREAT BRITAIN AND IRELAND), LIMITED.

Like football matches (below), air shows and aerobatic displays drew thousands of spectators to aerodromes around the country in the 1920s and 30s. H. M. Brock produced an appropriate image in 1927 for Player's Airman tobacco (opposite).

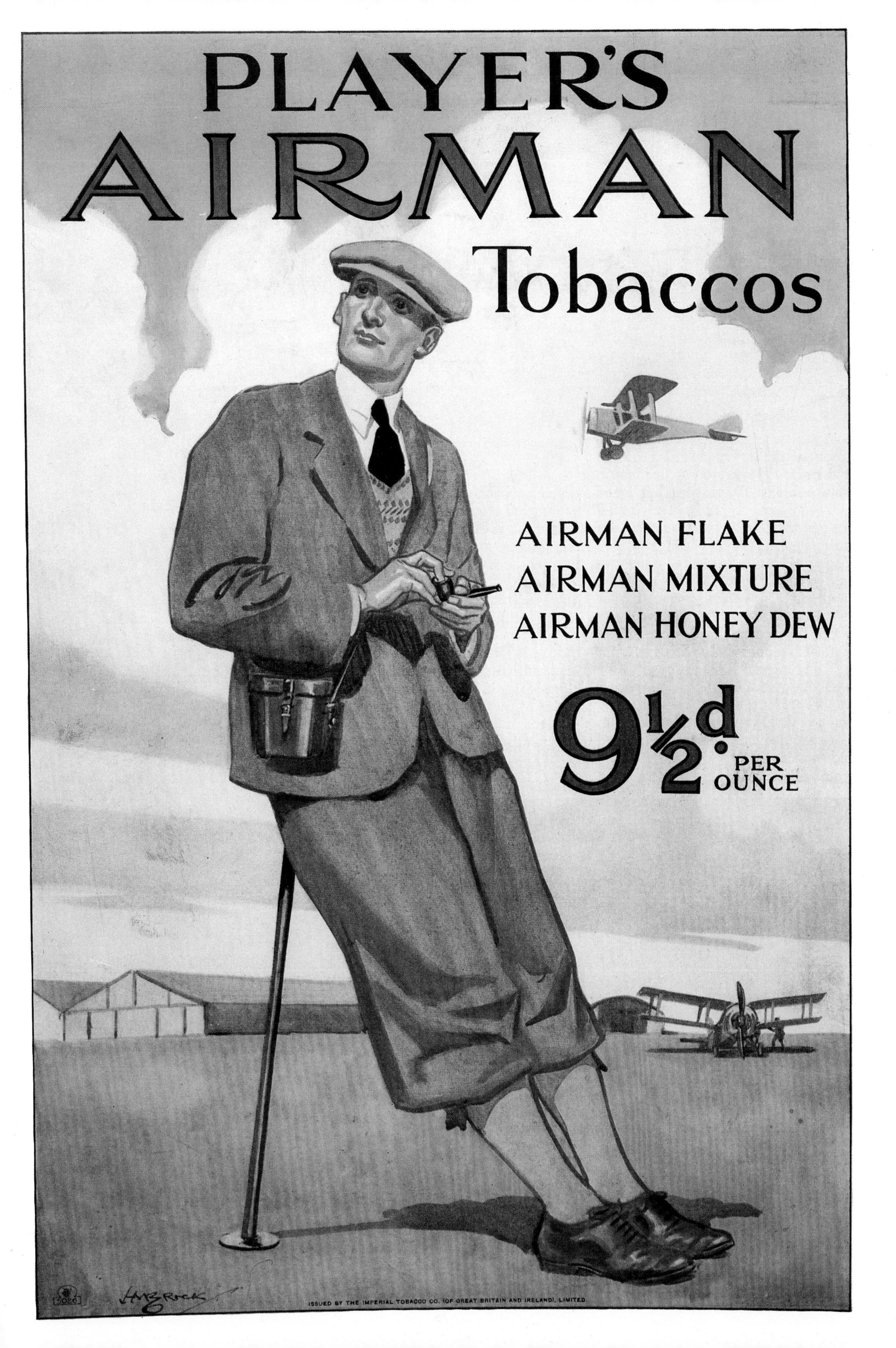
PLAYER'S
AIRMAN
Tobaccos
AIRMAN FLAKE
AIRMAN MIXTURE
AIRMAN HONEY DEW
9½d. PER OUNCE
5026
ISSUED BY THE IMPERIAL TOBACCO CO. (OF GREAT BRITAIN AND IRELAND), LIMITED.

Ogden's Coolie was not the easiest brand for which anything more than the most obvious visual imagery could be produced, but this winter scene of c. 1919 (opposite) gently brings out that quality of the tobacco embodied in the name. The relaxed, persuasively masculine air of this showcard and that for St Julien (below) would not have seemed out of place sixty years later.

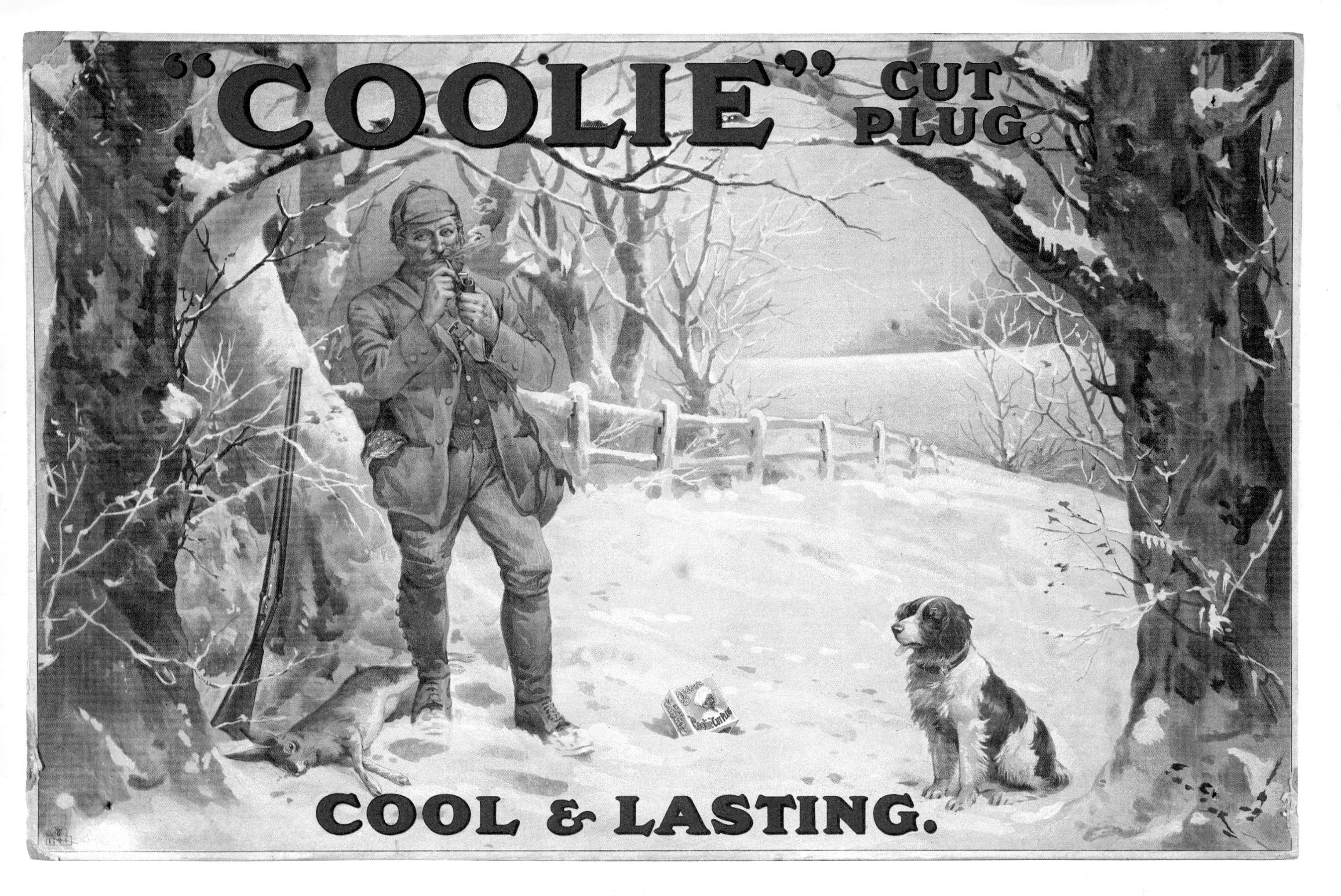
"COOLIE" CUT PLUG.
COOL & LASTING.

The East hinted at exotic fragrances and undreamed-of opulence, just the image needed to promote Coolie tobacco (opposite; a showcard of 1914) or Rajah cigars (below; from a 1910 edition of the *Daily Mail*).

OGDEN'S
"COOLIE" CUT PLUG.
Ogden's
"Coolie" Cut Plug
COOL &
LASTING.
"COOLIE"
CUT PLUG
2062
ISSUED BY THE IMPERIAL TOBACCO CO. (OF GREAT BRITAIN AND IRELAND), LIMITED.

## PIPE DREAMS

Two coincidentally similar designs for showcards appeared from Player's (opposite) ana Wills (below) in 1908 and 1909 respectively. Wireless was still a great novelty at the time, and it hit the headlines in a sensational way in 1910 when it played a crucial role in the arrest of the fleeing murderer Dr Crippen on board the SS *Montrose*.

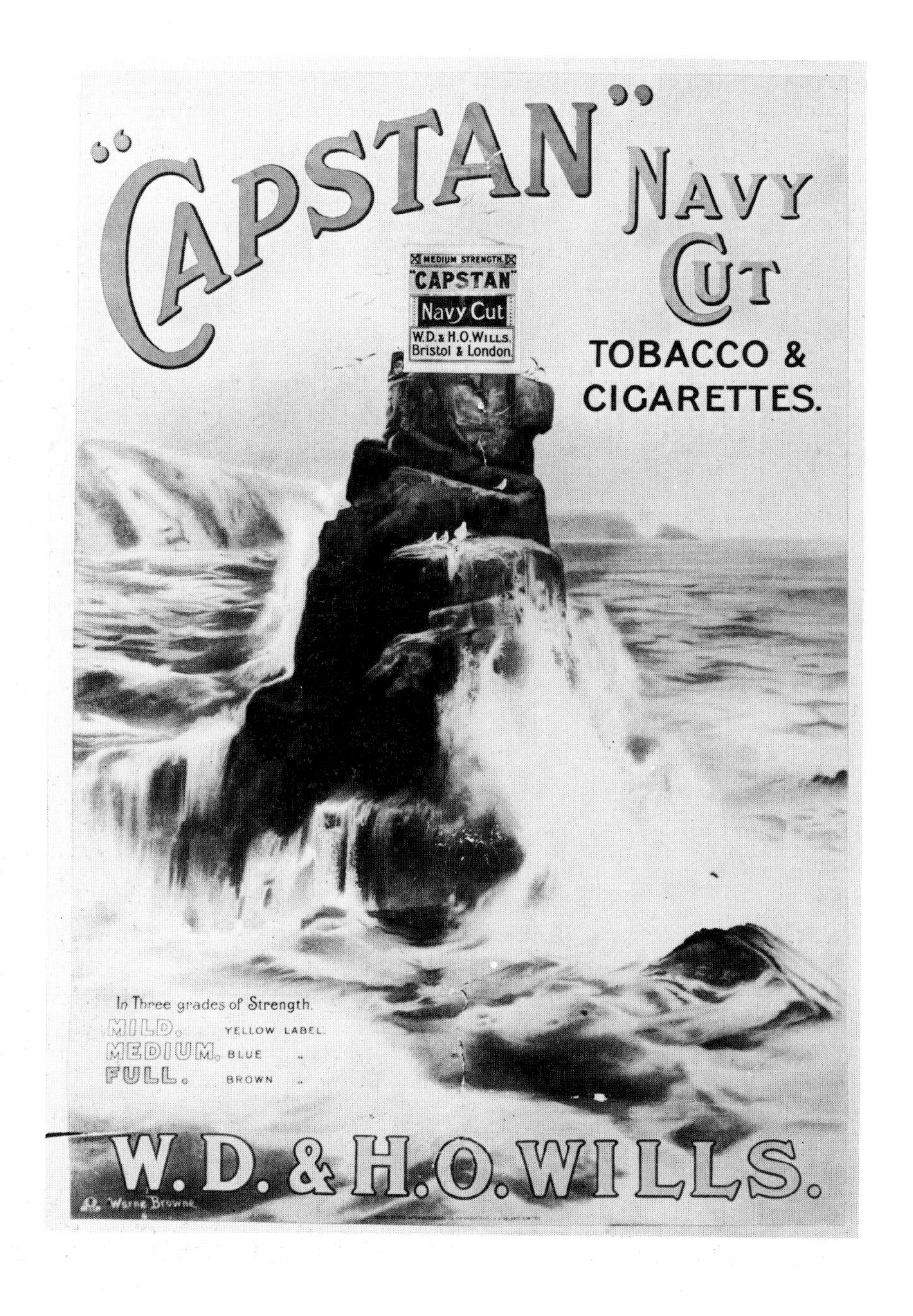

A WIRELESS MESSAGE:-

WE MUST HAVE

PLAYER'S

"TAWNY" NAVY CUT

TOBACCO

PLAYER'S
"TAWNY"
NAVY CUT

JOHN PLAYER & SONS.

CASTLE TOBACCO FACTORY, NOTTINGHAM.

ISSUED BY THE IMPERIAL TOBACCO CO. (OF GREAT BRITAIN & IRELAND) LIMITED.

Two generations of advertising. The wholly traditional showcard issued by Ogden's c. 1900 (opposite) is a cheerful design, marred by the illiterate pluralisation of the brand name; cigarettes with mouthpieces were a nine-day wonder in the tobacco trade at the time. Thousands of cards like this, covering a range of brands that ran into three figures, were produced between 1890 and 1940. By that time other forms of advertising were in the ascendancy: neon signs, cinema commercials and giant billboards, as well as street signs such as those displayed (below) at Brilliant Signs Ltd's London showrooms. Iron, glazed and illuminated signs and tablets can be seen; by the mid-1930s advertising was concentrating largely on the major brands.

Smoke

Ogdens TAB'S

5 Cigarettes and Mouthpieces

price 1D.

11.00.
DEPN. 2463

PLAYER'S
NAVY CUT.